START
BALANCING

START BALANCING

DEFINE YOUR SUCCESS.

LIVE WITH INTENTION.

BE HAPPY.

By Kristy Dickerson

Mom | Productivity Expert | Entrepreneur

START BALANCING

ISBN-10 0-9989972-0-9

ISBN-13 978-0-9989972-0-9

DEDICATION

To Tina, who showed me what grace and selflessness look like. Who fought a bigger battle and won.

See you again one day.

Tina Gayton Waldrop 1971–2011

I believe our dreams are worth chasing. I believe I was intended to fail, to struggle, and to face defeat in order to learn how to succeed. I have traveled across the country speaking, and teaching individuals how to start balancing and be productive. This book is a labor of love and I can't wait for you to read it! More importantly, I can't wait for you to make some changes and make things happen in your life!

Kristy Dickerson

1	Introduction
23	Know Yourself
39	Define Success
57	Be Accountable
67	Get Organized
89	Get Focused
97	Manage Your Time
111	Become Efficient
121	Establish Healthy Habits
135	Build Community and Relationships
143	Take Breaks
151	Overcome Obstacles
165	Hustle

YOU SHOULD NOT
HAVE TO CHOOSE
PROFESSIONAL OR
PERSONAL SUCCESS,
ONE OVER THE OTHER.

YOU CAN BALANCE THEM BOTH.

—KRISTY DICKERSON

#STARTBALANCING

INTRO

I love the word "start"—it's small but powerful, and it runs so deep for me. Start living, start hustling, start giving, start believing, start loving, start kickin' booty . . . sometimes you just have to stop thinking and START DOING! In this book I will not only walk you through the process of how to further define your purpose, but also give you the tools to help you succeed and find true happiness. When you have the ability to better balance your personal goals with your professional aspirations, anything is possible. Now, don't get me wrong, balance is a hard thing to maintain. It is something that requires constant work and refinement, as life will forever get in the way and throw obstacles in your path. As soon as you figure it out, the universe will force a change that you were not anticipating and life as you'd planned it will be disrupted. Everything you thought you had figured out will have to be reconfigured. This is where achieving balance becomes crucial.

I did not write this book because I have perfect balance or because I have it all together. If anything, I am going to share with you the mistakes I have made and what I have learned about business and about myself, in the hope that through my trials and tribulations—and the wisdom gained as a result—you will be able to *Start Balancing* a lot sooner than I did. I am an entrepreneur, a mom of three boys, and someone who has been able to leverage and grow a bootstrapped company fast. I didn't come from money and my solutions to a lot of challenges are not easy.

For the last ten years of my life I have been growing up, making mistakes, learning, and discovering what I need to "fill my cup up entirely." The key here is knowing who you are and what you need, then working and fighting every day to achieve it. Remember, the journey to your destination is long, so enjoy it. I am going to show you how to be productive along this journey we call life so you can be efficient with your time and so you can distribute your time where it matters most. The pages that follow are filled with actionable items that are applicable to your life and your goals. If you're ready for change, then let's keep going!

Nothing in life is ever given to you. You have to work, fail, be willing to pick yourself up and try again. Life is short, and the more effort you put into it, the more you will get out of it. It is up to you to craft the life that you want to live. You deserve to have success, to be purposeful, and ultimately to be happy—and I know you are ready to get started! You should seek to build a life that you don't feel the need to escape from. I believe that true happiness will come when you unlock your purpose in this world.

As human beings we all have a calling to be someone, to serve this world and the people who inhabit it in some way. I believe that our mission is to leave this world a better place than we found it. This sounds amazing, but how do we make this our day-to-day reality?

It's time to get control of your bills, your health, and your future. Whether your calling is to be a stay-at-home parent, to work in a corporate or nonprofit organization, or to start your own company, your goal should be to find your mission, harness it, and live. Perhaps you already know what you want to do, but your financial situation or other circumstances don't afford you the luxury. I've written this book to help you lay the path toward balancing your worlds and ultimately finding happiness and success regardless of where you are on your journey.

This book is not about my personal story, but rather about how what I have learned along the way can help you. These pages recount my journey and the journeys of others, and are a handbook to enable you to put into action the knowledge you will gain. They are the result of my opening up and taking an honest look in the mirror—at my life and myself. These pages are a candid and honest assessment of my growth, who I am, what I need to be happy, and what helped me to get there. I believe that this can be used as an example for your own self-discovery and I know that with application of these methods and with this newfound wisdom you can change your own life. These pages are an examination of what I am made of, how I have failed, and how I know you too will experience failure in some shape or form. This is the story of how I have succeeded at, struggled with, and prospered in the different pursuits along my personal path. I am not writing this book to give you simple answers to life's questions—I am not a person who was given an easy path to success. If you think that inadequate money or education, or health circumstances are holding you back, you're not going to find excuses in the pages of this book. What you will find instead is something more powerful—you will find that you can do anything you put your mind to. Because this is the truth: the only person who is holding you back is you. I know about failing and quitting. I understand the gut-wrenching tragedies that can suddenly or slowly shape us into the people we are today. But on the flip side, I know how hard work, and the success and freedom that follows, can shape the people we will become. Looking back, would I do anything differently? Of course! But I am also grateful for all of my experiences, good and bad, because they have made me who I am. Before we dive into solutions and action steps, here's a little about me.

I grew up in the small suburban town of Cumming, Georgia. The second child and the only girl in a family with three brothers, I had to learn from a very young age to be tough and competitive, and to stand my ground if I wanted to be heard, seen, and successful. I came from a middle-class family in which both my parents worked long, hard hours. My mother and father were hard workers whose success was directly impacted by their dedication and the quality of their work. My father owns a stonemasonry company and my mother owned a house-cleaning business. To this day, both of my parents are still working. It's part of who they are. Entrepreneurship gives you the ability to start a company and make money when you need it. It also allows you to start a business that complements your life, or to be someone who gives back and gains from your commitment to hard work and a better life. Entrepreneurship is also no easy path and you get out of it what you put into it, which sometimes means long hours, hard work, and weeks going by without a paycheck.

When I think about my younger years, I can see my elementary and middle-school self, red-faced and slinking my way out of my dad's work truck as he dropped me off at school. I was very aware of the loud shifting of gears and the obviousness of the old truck—I was afraid that the distinctive smell of dirt and concrete would stick to me and linger on my clothes all day in school, that someone would notice. The seats were lined with granules of rock; the engine rumbled with the changing of gears. I remember that my dad's lunch was always neatly packed away in the cooler at my feet. But more than that, I remember that I worried about what the look of that truck said about me. My situation felt different from that of the other children, whose parents, bedecked in suits and business attire on their way to more comfortable jobs or to spend their days volunteering, dropped them off in quieter and nicer cars. I felt different.

My dad was always dressed in blue jeans with mud stains on the knees and mud-caked work boots. My mother was forever in a baggy T-shirt, with no makeup, bleach-stained shorts, and a determined aura about the way she wrestled her day. I was embarrassed. I would tell my mom to make sure she was presentable before I'd let my friends see her. Yes, I know: shame on me for being embarrassed. The calluses on my parents' hands and knees are the result of the tireless hard work and sacrifices that they made so that my brothers and I would never be without anything afforded to other children. Even with their labor-intensive hours, neither of my parents ever missed an opportunity to be involved in my brothers' and my extracurricular activities: they were always there, always volunteering, always ready to lend a hand, a ride, or a valuable piece of advice. I am now ashamed that I was ashamed. My mother and father's work ethic was one of the most valuable life lessons I was lucky enough to learn. At the age of seven, I started my first job, taking out trash and vacuuming to help with the family business and to make a little money. Years later, I was the first in my family to graduate from college. It was during my time at Kennesaw State University that I developed my determination to find a mission in life that wasn't based solely upon the sweat of necessity, but rather, the implementation of what really makes me happy.

No college can teach you true work ethic, determination, and desire. When it comes to these qualities within me, I have nobody but my parents to thank. These priceless lessons are ones that I hope to pass down to my own children. I grew into the person I am with the understanding that nothing in life is ever just given to you. Hard, unrelenting work, and a clear visualization of your purpose are necessary for success. Leading by example is one of the best ways to teach this philosophy, and so here I am, writing this book to teach you what I know.

In high school I played sports while balancing my studies and multiple part-time jobs. I didn't have to work—my parents made sure of that. I chose to add work to my already full teenage schedule because I enjoyed the feeling of productivity and the excitement of juggling and succeeding in multiple aspects of my life at one time. Upon graduating from high school, my intrinsic desire to always be "something more" had developed, and I accepted a promotion to a managerial position with the company where I'd been working. I worked this new position while pursuing my degree in finance, and at the age of 18 I purchased my first house—a small, cozy town house on the outskirts of my college town, whose four walls represented for me far more than just a place to live. *The house was completely mine.* It was the first physical manifestation of my desire for that "something more." Here I was: young, independent, driven, and completely in control of my own destiny. The world was at my fingertips and the corporate ladder was mine to climb.

Looking back at this time in my life, there is a part of me that wishes I had been more carefree and not always so focused on getting to that next step. I had friends whose only worries at that age were sorority parties and how to get by with passing grades, and I look at them with admiration for being able to be fully present in that stage of life. For me, however, responsibility and working are, and have always been, the two things that wake me up in the morning and drive my passion for life. After I completed my freshman year and had managed to master the necessary skills for my employment at the time, my ambition to continue learning and growing once again took hold. I chose an educational path in finance because of my penchant for numbers and my knowledge that, if I could obtain this particularly difficult degree, success would surely follow.

During my sophomore year of college, I accepted a finance position with a local bank. There I was, moving forward in my life without a blueprint from my parents or any particular guidance about where I wanted to end up or how I would eventually get there. I didn't know it then, but I was already well on my way to building the foundation of my entrepreneurial dreams.

After working at the bank for a year, I met a young man (a customer) whose name was

Jeremy—you can imagine where this is going. He asked me for coffee and I politely said no. I was laser-focused on climbing the corporate ladder. I had my eyes on the prize—a life of purpose and happiness, without the burden of backbreaking labor to keep food on the table and a roof over my head. The man, however, kept coming back. For a full year, and against all odds, Jeremy persistently chased me. I turned down his efforts to court me until the day I walked to the office of my vice president, who, grinning, waved me in and shut the door.

It seems my suitor had not gone unnoticed, after all. The vice president had been quietly watching his valiant efforts to woo me and she had taken it upon herself to set the two of us up on a date. I wanted nothing to do with his or her efforts, but out of respect and kindness I told her I would give him one date. *One date.* I fell, and fell hard. It was only three weeks before we were engaged, and then another three months after that we said, "I do." In the fall of 2006 I became Mrs. Dickerson.

Yes, I know. *Who* does that? *Where* were the brakes? *What* had happened to that career-driven woman whose sole focus, whose single desire, was to be a champion in her career? Well, such is life. Sometimes life, and our perspective on why we are here, can change in the blink of an eye. As you look back on your own life, have you ever encountered someone or something that has drastically changed your plans?

Four months after we were married, in January of 2007, Jeremy woke up one cold, foggy morning with a horrific headache.

"Kristy, help!"

That cry for help was all I heard before I looked over and saw my husband having a grand mal seizure. At that moment, when I saw him shaking uncontrollably, his eyes rolled back, and foam around his mouth, my life was forever changed. My memory becomes a blur at that point—I called 911 and after what seemed like an eternity, the ambulance showed up and took him away.

A CT scan showed that Jeremy's brain was bleeding; he was airlifted to a trauma 1 center in northeast Georgia. Writing this, even now, it takes my breath away. Remembering those critical moments puts knots in my stomach and a ball of insecurities right back into my world. There I was, just beginning a life with this man—we were young, and we had big dreams—and suddenly tragedy struck and we were faced with an obstacle we didn't know how to face. The dreams were crumbling around us. *Why? Why me? Why him? Why us?* I asked it all.

As it turns out, Jeremy had a rare genetic blood-clotting disorder that we knew nothing about. Only a couple of months earlier I had married a confidant, successful (perhaps slightly cocky) man. Now I was checking out of the hospital with a husband with a newly diagnosed chronic disease and a desperate fear in his eyes. I was working to take care of Jeremy while trying to keep up with my studies. Looking back at myself during this portion of my life, I see a young woman on autopilot. I was depressed and seeking autonomy from the world. This was a deeply dark time in my husband's and my life. But we were lucky. Jeremy's brain stopped bleeding, the clots he was developing slowly dissolved, the seizures stopped, and the blood in his brain slowly reabsorbed. He was left with a condition that could be managed and treated with precaution and medications. We were lucky because even at its very worst, it was an illness that could be managed. From the outside, I seemed to have it all together. On the inside, I was a young woman with lingering insecurities about my husband, our life, and now myself. I was growing up faster than ever. Everything can change in the blink of an eye. This is a lesson I have learned all too well.

In the aftermath of my husband's diagnosis, it felt to me as though everything that had made me "Kristy" was gone. It was also at this time that my husband told me he wanted to start a family. I knew that I wanted to have children but I was still young and there was so much that I wanted to do—so many insecurities were at the surface. For the first time in my life, time seemed fleeting; I no longer knew if we had a lot of it. I was desperately looking for something permanent, some sort of security. It may seem like having a child at this point in time was a haphazard idea, but we decided to give it a shot. We were expecting right away.

Roman was our little miracle. He saved us in more ways than one. Since my husband's brain hemorrhage, all we had focused on was getting him well. Everything about Jeremy's medical issues was our top priority—we were in "fixing mode." And then, for the first time in our marriage we had something else to focus on, something that was good: our son. Soon after, I graduated with a degree in business finance and a minor in business management.

Now, though, I was faced with new questions. As a mother, could I leave Roman to pursue my own dreams? Would it be more appropriate to stay at home with my young son? Should I be a full-time stay-at-home mom? Could I still pursue a corporate career? As you can imagine, I was conflicted, but I knew I wanted to be someone. I needed an outlet to figure things out. I needed a place to let off steam and contemplate my next major decision. I quickly found that place in photography—an art that has always interested me.

Taking photographs was like therapy for me. Specifically, I threw myself into the pursuit of wedding photography. Capturing photos of couples on their wedding day brought me back to those fleeting, but happy, carefree newlywed days of my own. I jumped in with both feet. I went to workshops, I shot small sessions to pay for the cameras and supplies I needed, I went to conventions, and I started to feel alive again. I was ready to start something new. That "something new" became a full-on wedding photography business. It was a bumpy road, full of mishaps, but my business grew quickly. I networked, focused on PR, and was profiled in industry magazines numerous times. I shot some of the most lavish weddings, in and out of state. I felt alive and I felt like "Kristy" for the first time in a long time. I spent a good deal of time learning, traveling, connecting, growing, and becoming "me" again.

During this period of my life, wedding photography was the perfect outlet. It enabled me to shoot on the weekends and work from home during the week. After being in business for a couple of years and finally getting the hang of business ownership and being a mom of one, I felt the desire to grow our family. It didn't happen as easily as we'd expected and we had to turn to fertility treatments. Has there ever been something you desired that you could not have? Emotionally I was a wreck, and this affected all aspects of my life. With persistence, we welcomed a perfectly healthy boy—August, our wild man—in 2012 and to this day he has completely rocked our worlds. As a mom of two, everything that I had figured out was now off-kilter. My business was no longer flourishing like it had been because I didn't have as much time to dedicate to it. I now had a newborn and a preschooler, and I spent many of August's early days shedding tears wondering if I could handle both areas of my life. Could I be a mom and an entrepreneur?

Sure enough, I figured out I could and I got into the swing of things, being a mom of multiple kids and having a career. Three more years passed and a normal routine returned to my life and my business, and once again I wondered, "Is my family complete?" If we were going to have any more kids, now would be the time. Jeremy actually came to me first and said he wanted one more child, but with his career changing, he wasn't sure if it would be the best time. We knew we would have to have fertility treatments and it would take time, so we started the process. We got the disheartening news that our odds of conceiving were much lower this time. As time went on, life kept happening, and I wondered if maybe I wasn't supposed to have any more kids. We had fertility appointments on three different occasions, and for one reason or another we canceled them. In my heart, I became at peace with the idea that I was done and that maybe this was for the best. After returning from a girls' weekend, I wasn't feeling right. I thought I had a kidney or bladder infection but yes, as you have probably guessed, I was pregnant. We welcomed Silas in February of 2015 to complete our family.

During these years as a mother, a wife, and a professional wedding photographer, I experienced deep growth and understanding of myself, and learned to balance being a mother and a businesswoman. Through the trials and tribulations of life, I encountered failure, wasted money, and the experience of getting so far only to slip back to point A all over again. Until you face these losses and gains, and until you learn to continue onward, you really can't understand the true taste of success. I loved every second of this roller coaster because, through the rush of it all, I gained a sense of control over my destiny like never before. The challenge, thrill, and newness pushed me forward. I won't go into more detail of the companies I have started and ended along the way. Some were mediocre, some existed simply to generate passive secondary income, and some, in my eyes, were complete failures. For a long time, I allowed those failures, no matter how small, to define my ambition to press forward. Letting failure define your drive to succeed is a huge mistake.

Whether it is bad timing getting to the market, or poor investments made because of inexperience, every endeavor is a learning experience and nothing you do in the name of progress should ever be seen as a detriment. To paraphrase a common saying, *if you have never failed, it's because you've never tried anything new.*

In the interest of full disclosure, I must tell you that I have shed many tears trying to understand who I am and what I was meant to do. We all struggle with these life questions and the potential guilt that accompanies them as we look to fulfill our life's purpose. We cannot let the challenges, obstacles, or fear of failing determine our path. Where does this guilt come from? Our parents, society, or social media? Is it something we internalize for ourselves? I think it is a combination of all these things, and it is important that you find your purpose and come to an understanding that you are enough.

The struggle to be who we are meant to be—while being recognized as such—is a part of life that never truly goes away. A large part of my own growth happened while I was raising my children. During this process I learned who I was all over again. I relearned who I was while learning how to be a mother, wife, and friend to myself. I am still learning, breaking, and fixing my ways. We all want what is best for our families and we all dream of becoming the someone who we have always known we are meant to be.

The heartaches, trials, failures, and successes that have shaped me into the person I am today were the seeds that have sprouted into a business that aims to help everyone with a desire to succeed. After four years of wedding photography I started teaching in my industry. I had the rare combination of being in a creative field and holding a finance degree, so I started helping others turn their creative passions into businesses. In the spring of 2015, I reached out to a graphic designer, Jenny Grumbling, who I asked to design a few pages of my business content, with the hope of someday turning it into a teaching book. She mentioned to me that she really wanted to create a planner. Thus, the idea of STARTplanner was born.

At this time, I had a two-month-old and two older kids, and a husband who was back in school—you know, the ideal time to start a business. I can't explain my decision, except to say that I just knew this was a path I was supposed to take, despite not being the "ideal" time. This was my purpose. It felt right and I knew this tool would change lives because I knew that the struggles I was facing, others faced as well. Not to downplay this experience, as it was not easy, but within six months of the launch of STARTplanner, and with no cash invested, we were able to produce six-figure sales, and Jenny and I were able to pursue our dreams full time. Through my work with STARTplanner and keynote speaking, I achieved some major bucket-list goals by being featured on notable sites such as *Entrepreneur*, Inc. com, and *Forbes*, among others. Yes, this is a validation of my ideas and myself, but more importantly, it is an example to show you that you can do this too.

Looking back on my life, I think everything I went through brought me to this particular moment of professional success—and if you look at your life you can find the same pivotal moments happening in your life. For me, it was those moments of failure and struggle that truly changed and pushed me, both personally and professionally. Everything that I had learned about branding, delegation, efficiency, and business really came together with the perfect partner and resources to make it happen. I had every reason not to pursue this passion, as I already had three kids and a thriving business. I felt compelled to follow my heart, as I always had. My husband was confused as to why I wanted to pursue something else, but he reluctantly supported my new endeavor. I was being prepared to do something bigger in this world than I was aware. I have found that my mission is to help others to be productive and inspire them to find happiness, balance, and their passion in life—this has always been part of who I am. I knew I had to do this.

STARTplanner is a planning tool that can help you achieve goals and financial freedom, and bring organization to your life and business, while saving you time and money. The planner is the first of its kind to have financial planning content for your home life, as well as a small business if you have one. It helps you organize your goals, monitor your healthy habits (gym visits and water intake), plan meals throughout the week, and prep for trips to the grocery store. It also has sections allotted for planning your vacations, holidays, and more. You are given the organizational tools to make planning life easier, from everything you thought you needed to plan to things you didn't even know you needed! We have received countless emails from people whose lives have been changed by STARTplanner. Our planner has brought peace, order, direction, organization, and balance into their daily worlds. I truly believe that in order to find success, you have to focus on all aspects of your life, not just one, and this is what STARTplanner does.

I use STARTplanner so that my children's sports schedules and our social lives can be gracefully organized and intertwined into my work schedule and business arrangements, ultimately giving my worlds balance. To me, there is nothing more powerful than having a tool that allows me to visualize, plan, and execute for success in all aspects of my life. Whether you plan and organize on paper, with apps, or online, it is important that you do it consistently.

Life is a constant balancing act. Each of us in our own personal way goes through the ups and the downs of life. I believe I was meant to have a difficult journey so that I would know how to help others manage and flourish during theirs. What I realized while traveling and teaching about productivity, balance, and the idea of success is that this is something we all battle with. I was coaching a recent graduate, Jaime, who'd studied cinematography and whose goal was to own her own company and produce commercials and amazing creative videos. She was young, very talented, and a hard worker. What she was missing was the business knowledge to put together a solid brand to attract ideal clients. Her website was rebranded and I coached her on workflows and processes. Within six months of rebranding, she was approached by a very well-known, reputable company that wanted Jaime to join its team. Her original goal was to be an entrepreneur but she had realized that she hated the business aspect and she really wanted to focus on what she loved doing most, which was shooting. Had we not rebranded Jaime's business and taken her through this entire process, would she have discovered this? Would she ever have been viewed as an asset to that company where she was offered her dream job?

Another individual I recently coached had a personal training and coaching business. She had been in business for more than four years and she was buried in work. After talking with her, a few things stood out to me: she was burned out, she was not making money like she should have been, and she was so busy working in her business that she hadn't taken any time to work on her business. I saw major gaps where she could have been automating processes. She needed to make her brand and the products offered clearer; and she needed to delegate or outsource in order to focus her attention on her strengths. It sometimes takes an outside perspective to see gaps or areas that can be improved upon, which can literally change your life. Sometimes you are so close to a situation that you cannot see everything. Do I have business advisors, mentors, and consultants for my business? Absolutely.

The other day, I had lunch with a friend who had recently graduated, and who has been at her current job for just over a year. She loves what she is doing but she also doesn't feel like she is being used to her full potential. She really likes the company she works for, but she doesn't see any room for moving up the corporate ladder any time soon. She also works a lot of hours, which digs into her personal life, and she doesn't feel like she has boundaries, or *could* have boundaries, for that matter. I told her to put her resume together, ask for a meeting with her boss to let him know her concerns, and to start looking for other jobs. I advised her, "That company might not even know you are unhappy. They might also have positions opening up, and you will not be on their radar if they don't know you are eager." You should always keep your resume, business headshots, and LinkedIn profile up-to-date. Never stop networking and pushing yourself forward. Change is scary, but if there are no potential openings where my friend currently is, then she needs to start looking for another job. No one is ever going to give you permission to push yourself forward. Change is not always easy, but you deserve happiness and you have a unique set of skills that is of value to this world.

I recently consulted for someone who ran a gym. He felt that what really made him shine, and the core of what made the company go around, was his story and his motivating demeanor. Everything he had built was running autonomously, and I suggested he start developing a brand around his name. Why didn't he start speaking and motivating others in his field? I saw his eyes light up. It was as if he knew that was what he should do, but he needed someone else to see it and believe it. We hold ourselves back in so many ways. We doubt ourselves, and we need a tribe of people to push us forward.

Jenny, my business partner at STARTplanner, has a life that looks very different from mine; she is a single mom of one. When I approached her about this idea of creating a company, she had recently left a 9-to-5 job with a company where she'd felt undervalued, and had started her own company. She was struggling to figure out if that was the right thing for her or if she would find another job. There were so many things about entrepreneurship that she hated, especially the business aspects and financials. She had so many goals that were sitting stagnant, and her personality leads her to take small steps and process things before taking action. I am the opposite—I don't think, I just act, which may explain why so many things in my life happened so fast. I knew that if we started our company I would not only be assuming responsibility for her but for her son as well, and I knew we only had one shot. Promises were not going to put food on the table or give her the necessities that she needed. I knew she was my counterbalance and the strength to my weaknesses.

Last but not least, my husband Jeremy was an example. He started a company at the age of 20, and in 2012 he had an opportunity to sell it. His entrepreneurial spirit had diminished and ultimately he figured out that he no longer wanted to carry the responsibilities that a company of that magnitude required. Also, through his health diagnosis he had developed an interest in medicine. In 2012, he came home one day and said he wanted to pursue a lifelong dream of going to college, get a four-year degree, and become a nurse. Accomplishing this was no easy feat—his wife was an entrepreneur, he was in his mid-thirties, and he had three children. Jeremy graduated with that degree in 2017 and is now starting a career as an ICU nurse. It is never too late to chase your dream and it is a process to find your purpose.

These struggles are things we all face. There have been times when I wanted to quit, when I couldn't figure things out, and when I physically could not pursue endeavors. There have been times that my world was so off balance I felt my life was spinning out of control. I know and can recognize a lot of the struggles that others are going through, because I have been through them as well. We all struggle with fear, change, or ourselves to different degrees at different points in our lives. Balance is not an easy thing. Being organized, efficient, and constantly pushing yourself forward is not always easy. No matter where you currently are in your life, seeking balance and fulfillment will be a lifelong pursuit. It is a process, and one that you should never give up on.

Did you read this introduction and think, *I am so different from her?* We are all different and uniquely designed. I myself often feel "different" or feel that I don't fit in. But these principles apply to us all. I know that if you read on, you will be able to take away tips and lessons, and have the ability to change your life. In the following pages you are going to uncover layers of discovery for yourself. Every chapter has accompanying worksheets, so you will not just be reading, you will be learning, doing, and planning to make things happen. I am going to show you solutions to help you find the clarity to get busy defining success, finding your purpose, and being happy. I'll give you solutions for making more time for intentional moments, by being more productive and efficient with your time. If your intentions are to make progress on your dreams, put thought into action, and find a more productive and accomplished version of yourself, I encourage you to read on. You deserve to be happy and we are going to make things happen together!

BE HAPPY

#**START**BALANCING

ONE

KNOW YOURSELF

We are all different. We are all uniquely created with skills and experiences that I believe have a purpose in this world. In the introduction, I felt like it was important to show you who is filling these pages with content. I felt like I needed you to understand where I came from, the obstacles I have faced, and that I did not write this book because I have it all figured out. I am *not* always balanced. I have walked these experiences, have faced obstacles, and have found out what it takes for me to push my life forward. I wrote this book because I have knowledge, experience, and time-saving information to share and I know that, with application, the content within these pages to come will change your life!

Before we take any steps forward I want to start by asking you to take a look in the mirror at who you are, at what makes you tick—at your strengths, your weaknesses, and your own journey—and learn to be thankful for it. Knowing oneself is a process, and typically we find out who we are as we are growing up. Knowing ourselves takes time, and it is no easy feat. We are constantly changing and growing, and I can assure you that continuing to develop who you are will be a lifelong pursuit.

When I was growing up, I wanted to be a lawyer. I saw lawyers in their sleek suits, looking so important and smart. I knew I wanted more out of life and I was willing to go through the education and struggle to get myself there. During college (while studying corporate law) I became intrigued by the stock market. Soon after, I started reading *The Wall Street Journal* every day and doing some day trading. In the WSJ, I saw articles about women who were making waves in the business world and I thought to myself, *that could be me one day.*

My final semester in college, I had a professor who taught small-business management. This class really piqued my interest; I read all the books the professor suggested. During this class we were able to run a business via a simulator. I had to figure out and understand cost of goods sold, return on investment, profit and loss, and how it all played into marketing,

PR, and accounting. I loved it! My company that semester was the most profitable during the class, until I made a risky move and lost it all. This particular instructor was a wealth of knowledge, as he had owned several companies, sold them, retired, and decided to go into teaching to share all he had learned. The other business professors were always dressed to a T and drove nice cars. He was different. He wore nice enough clothes, and he drove a perfectly middle-class car that looked to be at least ten years old.

One afternoon I stayed after class to ask him some questions about his life and businesses, because I was so intrigued. After talking with him I discovered that he was probably one of the wealthiest instructors on campus although you wouldn't know it by looking at him or the car he drove. I asked him about his car and he said, "Why would I invest my own personal already taxed money on a nice car, when it is nothing but a depreciating asset? And why would I give all of my talents to a company to build their dreams when I know I am capable of building my own dreams?" That conversation changed me and it made me literally redefine what success meant in my own life.

That semester, I decided I was no longer going to be a lawyer, or someone who did day trading on Wall Street, or someone who climbed a corporate ladder—I wanted to create my own company. I didn't have a clue in the world what it would be, but that was my dream. My earlier aspirations had just been mere ideas of what I thought looked appealing, but I was at a point in my life where I really did not know what I was good at or what I would even enjoy. If you are still at that point in your life, shadow others, get an internship, or talk to someone in the profession you're interested in. Sometimes your dreams get put on hold when bigger things happen, but you should still try to figure out what your dreams are. As you've read, my husband had a health problem and life unfolded like it did, not according to any of my plans. I felt like my life was no longer mine to live, but that I was clinging to hope and normalcy.

Suddenly, everything changed. That is the tricky part of dreams. Once you decide what you want to do, life will often come in and throw you a curveball. In my case, there were multiple curveballs: my husband's medical condition; my choice to pursue owning a business and being a mom; and the decision to walk away from one career that I loved to start another that I felt called to do. Often, unexpected events in your life define not only your path, but also who you become. They shape your passions and define what is important to you and how you measure success. Do you know what I did after my husband had his brain hemorrhage, and we had spent countless nights in the hospital? I kid you not, I went back to my college campus and met with my counselor to determine what additional courses I would need in order to go to medical school. I wanted to fix my husband and to fix others who were in his shoes. I didn't pursue that path, but I want to remind you that good and bad things will happen in your life—if you're lucky, more good than bad—and I believe these events will mold you into who you are meant to be. Looking back over my journey, had any of it been different I wouldn't be the person pursing the passions that I am today, so I wouldn't change a thing.

The reason I'm telling you all this is not to say that life is hard or dreams will get sidelined, or that you might have to change the path of your dreams. I am telling you all this because this is how growth happens. You might still be in the discovery phase or you might be in a phase of feeling stuck. We grow the most when we are forced to endure failure, obstacles, or tragedies. This is how life impacts us—shaping us into who we are in this world. That time in my life—my husband's medical issues, my believing I was going to become a doctor—was a two-year period. As you can imagine, over the last ten years those kinds of scenarios have been endless for me, with pursuing different passions and raising a family. Read the biographies of any great self-made leader or businessperson and you'll find the same story. No one got where they are without challenges along the way. It's like climbing a mountain—the closer you get to the top, the more challenging it is, the thinner the air,

SUCCESS LIES IN PERSEVERANCE.

—KRISTY DICKERSON

#STARTBALANCING

the rockier the earth, and the more likely the path is to be worn away or confusing or nonexistent. This is where people either become successful or do not. Success lies in perseverance; it is the decision to press forward through the hard times, keeping your vision and goals clear. I don't think this part ever stops, and you will constantly encounter things in your life, both good and bad, that will affect who you are. People, circumstances, and tragedies will affect everyone. I believe this is all for a reason and a bigger purpose. You might not see it that way when you are in the thick of it, but I believe that everything does happen for a reason. If you are currently in a bad place in your life, please believe it is for a greater purpose. Hang on, believe, and keep pressing on.

Both business and life are about knowing and understanding people. You have to know yourself first, and then you have to know others. To find success, you must know who you are in order to align yourself with individuals who can help get you there by being able to fill in your weaknesses with their strengths. Everyone has different motivations for working. For some it is money, for some it is to have a purpose, and for others it is a responsibility. Knowing your own motivations and recognizing others' will give you the greatest chance for success.

You need to be able to identify your own strengths and weaknesses. From a strengths standpoint, you should pinpoint and look honestly at what you are good at and (on the other side of that coin) what you are not good at. Just because you have weaknesses doesn't mean you won't be able to achieve your dreams. One of my biggest technical weaknesses is grammar and writing, and one of my biggest weaknesses from a business perspective is not being able to give up control. I have a hard time trusting that others will get the job done the way I want it done. I have a tendency to try to do everything myself. Did I pretty much just say I was a control freak? Yes, in general terms! Yet I am writing this book and continuing to trust, teach, and delegate tasks to others because I know that where I have weaknesses, there are others far greater than me who can do the task better, and this dream wouldn't be realized otherwise. Because you know what? I know for certain that although my name is on this book and my thoughts and ideas fill these pages, I didn't create it alone because we are not designed to be good at everything. Sometimes knowing your weaknesses is the greatest strength of all.

Understanding your weaknesses allows you to grow both personally and professionally in order to make things happen. If you spot a grammatical error in this book I will be pointing the finger to someone else because I delegated that task. You see the beautiful cover design and graphics throughout? I didn't do that. I knew I had a calling to write a book to share these tips and my life's experiences in order to inspire others, but I also knew I couldn't do it alone. I had a clear vision of a self-help book that focused on how to be productive in order to *Start Balancing*. I knew from an aesthetic perspective I wanted the book to have a clean, modern design. Although it might not stand as thick as other business books, I intentionally wanted the text to be straightforward so that it would authentically convey my message as precisely as possible. I wanted the book to be square to indicate that it is different from the other books on the shelves, evenly proportioned to represent balance, and concise and practical to be considerate of your time. I wanted quotations to appear throughout the book to be encouraging and to keep you inspired, and I wanted you to feel as if I were reading the book with you. I had a very clear vision of what I wanted *Start Balancing* to be, and I knew I couldn't make it happen alone. If I, someone whose single biggest weakness is grammar, can write a book, that right there should be a lesson that with knowledge and a clear vision you can do anything! You just need to know yourself, understand what you are good at, and then find resources to help you with your weaknesses.

Now don't get stuck on weaknesses. Be willing to list all your strengths! Some of them will be major, and some of them may (at first) seem inconsequential. I know my strengths: I am a numbers gal, I'm a visionary, I understand operations, I can problem solve quickly, I am competitive, I like leading others, and my motivator is not money but responsibility and purpose. If you're unsure of your own strengths, I encourage you to take a personality test to help you understand yourself more. I have suggested a few of these tests at the end of the chapter.

When assessing your strengths and weaknesses, have you uncovered a passion? Is there something that keeps you up at night? Is there a cause or a benefit for the greater good that you are passionate about? It might be a product, service, or a personal strength that you have tapped into. If you know what you're passionate about, you are one of the lucky ones. Harness this knowledge and apply it. That doesn't mean you need to own a business. I am an entrepreneur and I know entrepreneurship is a passion of mine. Owning a business is not for everyone, and you can use your strengths in other pursuits to become a force to be reckoned with. Knowing what you are passionate about is half the battle; finding some way to utilize your strengths is the second part.

Failure doesn't keep us from success; fear of failure does. I don't care how old you get or how much knowledge you gain—fear is still there and is a very real thing. It is something you just have to learn to control. Experience, knowledge, and a support team will help you lessen those fears. I want to be frank when I say this: *the reality is that you might fail.* You might have already failed. I have started companies that have been nothing shy of mediocre. I have poured countless ideas into projects that didn't pan out for one reason or another. For a long time, I used my failure as a reason to not press forward. I let that hold me back and define me, thinking, *if I do something else, will I fail?* Failure or the fear of it can stop you in your tracks. Failure is part of success, and you only truly fail if you give up. But which is worse: trying and failing, or never trying? To me the fear of never trying at all is worse. To me, chasing a dream is just as necessary as breathing oxygen. I don't feel fully alive or purposeful if I am not reaching for my calling.

FAILURE DOESN'T KEEP US FROM

SUCCESS;

FEAR OF FAILURE DOES

—KRISTY DICKERSON

#STARTBALANCING

NO ONE ELSE
IS EVER GOING TO
GIVE YOU PERMISSION
TO CHASE
YOUR DREAMS.
—KRISTY DICKERSON

#STARTBALANCING

Looking back over my journey I know hands-down that failure has stopped me from pursuing certain things. The older, wiser version of me knows that those failures were only failures if I let them be defined as such. I now see them as stepping-stones for my personal and professional growth. The challenges I have faced and the bad decisions I have made have helped me grow far more than my successes have. If you operate with the mind-set that you might fail, focus on past mistakes, or fear of what others will think, you might as well quit. Being bold and brave is not easy, but the bolder you are, the more opportunities you will have. Period.

Knowledge is power. The more informed you are about the situations you encounter, in life and business, the better you will become at making decisions and tucking fear away. Constantly seek knowledge and try to better understand yourself by reading business books and self-help books, furthering your education, or attending seminars or workshops. It is also okay to pursue something for a while and decide it is not worth pursuing anymore. No one else is ever going to give you permission to chase your dreams or say it is okay if your dream has changed—only you can do that. Only you can decide whether fear will control you or you will control it. You have to push that fear aside and not only say that you can achieve your goals, but believe that you can!

Is being an entrepreneur right for you? Is managing a household right for you? Is volunteering? What about going back to school? Are you someone who doesn't need or want to follow a blueprint? Or would you thrive being under someone else's direction and being able to do what you love most? Should you work from home or would you find more success at a 9-to-5 job that you're able to leave behind at the end of the day? Should you work in corporate America? Independently? Should you become a parent? Should you start that other company? Understanding and knowing yourself helps to answer all of these questions while aligning them with your goals. I meet a lot of people who have basically set themselves up for failure. They are hustling, but not quite sure what their next steps are; they haven't utilized self-knowledge as a tool to make their dreams come to fruition. You also may be at a point in your life where you are doing your current job not because you love it because you have to. Of course you need the money, but these tools and lessons will help to move your life in the direction of your dreams. It is also important to note that often you may not be "ready" for those next steps in life—but when are we *ever* fully ready to dive in and make a change? You just have to be willing to roll up your sleeves, figure it out, and move forward confidently in the direction of your dreams.

Here is a scenario of discovery. Sarah goes to art school and studies interior design. Her dream is to run her own design studio. She graduates and starts investing in a space and the resources that she needs. She starts taking on various jobs to help bring in a little income. Her passion and strength are in decorating and connecting with customers, but she now finds herself crunching numbers, working 80 hours a week, and trying to figure out how to run her business. Success to her had meant running her business, but after discovering who she is and what her strengths are, success now means working for an interior design company or partnering with someone who loves design but has a strong business sense. This way she can focus on what she loves and let someone else run the business side.

Knowing who you are, the person who lies deep within, is important, and this can change often. The person you aspire to be is one of the hardest people to know. If you are still figuring out what you want to do when you grow up, you're not alone. For a lot of people this is a lifelong process. What I do know now, after years of work and personal struggles and triumphs, is myself. I have learned who I am, what works for me, and what doesn't.

I know what I need to feel fulfilled on a daily basis, and that is what I am going to focus on to be happy, free, and successful. I want you to find the same happiness, freedom, and success. Take personality tests and ask the people in your life about you. If you are married, ask your spouse—I promise they won't hesitate to answer! Life will constantly happen, and everything you thought you were will constantly be reassessed. Here is the truth of the matter: no matter how hard it seems, no matter how out of touch with yourself or your dreams you might become when life and responsibility for others become overwhelming, you are worth fighting for. You were meant to do something purposeful and powerful. YOU are a beautiful creation and not only were you *meant* to succeed, but you *deserve* to succeed.

Let's take a moment to take a good look at ourselves. The worksheets on the following pages will help us to understand who we are.

GETTING TO KNOW **YOU**

MY OVERALL STRENGTHS

_____

_____

_____

MY OVERALL WEAKNESSES

_____

_____

_____

CHANGES TO IMPLEMENT IN THE NEXT 30 DAYS

☐ _____

☐ _____

☐ _____

WAYS TO CONTINUE EXPANDING MY KNOWLEDGE

PERSONALITY ASSESSMENT RESULTS
(I.E. GALLUP ASSESSMENT, MYERS-BRIGGS TEST, STRENGTHSFINDER)

TWO

DEFINE SUCCESS

Will I ever be "successful?" Will I ever be happy in my profession and feel valued? Should I go to college? Should I start a family? Can or should I work if I have children? Will I ever get married and find a life partner? I hate my day job; will I ever be able to quit and work from home? If I pursue this business venture, can I make it profitable or will I fail? Will I be wasting my time? What if I take all this time away from my kids and it's for nothing? Can I get that new job opportunity? Can I lose weight and hold myself accountable? Can I rest my head at night knowing that I gave it my all today, that I was the best version of myself as a parent, as a spouse, as a friend, and as a son or daughter? Am I enough? Will I ever see myself as successful?

Do the questions above sound at all familiar? As working individuals in today's world, so many of us grapple with knowing the right way to achieve a healthy balance between personal and professional success. Sometimes we don't even know if professional success is possible, or worth it. Here's a question for you: what does success look like to you? Is it to work from home, or perhaps to work part time? Is it to start a family and be the primary caregiver for the kids? If you're reading this book, it is likely you want to do both. You want to be fulfilled by pursuing your professional passions without sacrificing your personal pursuits. What do you need in order to feel you've realized your dream? Flexible hours? Total autonomy? Financial freedom? Maybe it's something you are still figuring out. Is your heart's desire to start a new business doing something you love? Is it to work for a nonprofit on a mission that is near and dear to your heart? Perhaps you don't care what the business is, as long as it pays for the life you picture yourself living. I meet so many people who, while they are hustling and working as hard as they can, are still left feeling like success eludes them. But when I ask those very same people what success looks like to them, they very often describe their life in its current state, or not too far from it. But if you are successful and don't feel like you are, you've missed the point. On the other hand, some people describe a life so unattainable with their current resources that they're setting themselves up for failure. They don't know what to do or how to start. That's where I come in—to show them how to get unstuck and be brave enough to dream attainable dreams. I am going to show you that it is possible to make things happen, to be professionally accomplished, and to maintain a social life.

We live in a society in which individuals have the desire to pursue their dreams, but often don't know how to approach these dreams or where to start. Your life either gets filled with events and you end up heading in another direction than you intended, or you stand on an unclear path, feeling lost and confused. We also live in a world of comparisons—and we shouldn't. Measuring who you are and what you do against anyone else is toxic to your morale and in no way sets you up to succeed. There is no universal definition of success. Your success is completely different from everyone else's and your mind-set is the first thing you have to change. We have this illusion that success means go to college, get a good job (or start a business), buy a house, get married, travel, have a baby, get a new car, have another baby, move into a bigger house, and the story continues. Let me ask you this: if you are successful but you don't feel it, does it matter? We all have different benchmarks of how we measure our success as well. Success could be measured with money, fame, appearance, intelligence, or anything else you use as a standard. I personally think success should be measured on well-being: your ability to be content with who you are, feel authentic happiness, and fill your life with intentional moments. It is up to each of us to define success, and I think it is paramount that you take a moment to do this, write it down, and put it somewhere so you will see it often.

We tend to define success or goals once a year, in the form of a New Year's resolution. An independent study by Statistic Brain showed that 41 percent of Americans typically make New Year's resolutions, and of that only 9.2 percent feel they were successful in achieving their goals.[1] The inability to find success causes stress.

According to a recent survey conducted by Gallup, "Most Americans sometimes experience stress in their daily lives, including 4 in 10 who say they encounter it frequently. Parents of younger children, working Americans, and younger Americans are most likely to report enduring time pressures and stress."[2] I'll tell you exactly how those stressed and unsuccessful individuals are feeling—I know because I've been there. They feel as if the pursuit of one is at the sacrifice of the other.

Maybe you work too hard at a day job and think it comes at the expense of time with your family in the evening. You decide to leave your job and stay home with your kids but miss your job. Maybe you're in your mid-twenties and you want to advance your career, so you start job hunting and get offered a new job. You leave the comfort and safety of your first career to push yourself forward. The new job comes with travel, learning, and requires more time. You feel as if there is not enough time or enough of you to go around. Or you love your children too much to sacrifice time with them for a pipe dream that has no guarantee of success. Maybe you are doing big things with your career but you feel at times that you are sacrificing time with your family, your friends, or your children. Or are you at the opposite end of the spectrum? Have your kids graduated and moved out, leaving you with a slower-paced life, unsure what to do with your time? Are your kids in school, so you are looking for something to do part time?

Not having a clear path or balanced worlds leads to stress or a feeling of not being useful or fulfilled. I firmly believe that true happiness and fulfillment comes when you are able to use your talents to help a cause or for a greater good, without sacrificing other aspects of your life. I believe that you can and should follow your dreams and pursue your definition of success. In not following your dreams, you do yourself and your family an injustice by not living up to your full potential—your happiness will suffer. There is a reason why people have "lingering dreams" and "nagging ideas": people have an undeniable need to pursue their passions and find happiness through achievement. They feel stagnant and unfulfilled when they ignore that inner voice that continues to ask those nagging "what if" questions. Personal success doesn't have to come at the expense of professional success, and vice versa.

Lack of balance is a widespread epidemic that is affecting our society, and this can lead to stress, health repercussions, and a life of poor time management that means missing out on your own life. Time is the one and only thing we cannot get back, and is one of the hardest things to manage. Balance is a hard thing to achieve and it can affect working adults, parents, and virtually anyone who is pursuing a life to better themselves.

For you, the definition of success (and your ultimate goal) might be to be able to stand on your own two feet. It might be to become the primary caregiver of your children. Success for you might mean being the breadwinner and providing for your family in a financial way. Or success might be something between these two goals. Have you set a realistic way to measure this success in a quantitative form? Have you really stopped and thought about this? Have you written it down? Wherever you are in your life, and whether or not you have kids, you are always going to have multiple goals. This is where the juggling act takes place. Let's face it: no matter what, you will still have to learn to balance your personal and professional ambitions.

Over the years, my idea of what success means has vastly changed. I used to think success was when I could go to work in Corporate America, sporting a sharp suit daily, taking expense-account lunches, and earning a decent living. Now I look at that one-time goal of success and think *entrapment!* Confinement to someone else's schedule at someone else's desk would be my ultimate demise, a kind of slow torture. On the contrary, for some, the responsibility of running a company might be their own agony. Working for yourself does allow for more flexible hours and can help you to more easily balance your worlds. It can also set you up to give only 50 percent of who you are to each pursuit, if you do not properly manage your time. I would never want to be confined to someone else's rules in the workplace, but that was once my dream. We change, and we grow. Your definition of success and goals should be reassessed often because your definition of success will change as you grow. Events will happen and circumstances in your own life will change that will slightly shift the way you see things, and my hope for you is that at the end of this book you will do just that: see things differently. We are all built for different reasons and part of growing and learning about yourself is figuring out in which environment or on what path you'll thrive. If you have not already written down what success looks like for you, we are going to be doing just that at the end of this chapter! Don't worry about it being perfect or about knowing what the "end" looks like; just put pen to paper to solidify your dreams. The key is getting started. Every dream has to start somewhere.

In order to know where you are going and how to make a plan to get there, you have to define what success looks like, and you will be able to do this better once you know yourself. Once you know what success looks like and how you plan to measure it, you should create goals for all aspects of your life—this is an important step that you cannot skip. Success happens when you meet a goal. You should set overall goals that govern your life and your decisions about how to spend your time. You'll want to define success both in broad terms and quantifiable forms for different areas of your life. For example, if your goal is to start a new business, your broad terms could be "I want to start a new business offering health coaching." Then make it more quantifiable: "I will open the company in February and my goal is to turn a profit, making $5,000 a month by the end of the year so I can leave my day job." You will have to revisit this on a regular basis because, I assure you, it will change.

You're going to be writing down what success is and aligning your goals for both your professional and personal life. The goals you set for yourself should be SMART goals:

SPECIFIC: Clearly define what you want to achieve.

MEASURABLE: Determine how to quantify your achievements for this goal.

ATTAINABLE: Is this something that can be achieved?

REALISTIC: Is this something that can be achieved given your resources and time?

TIME-BASED: Always give yourself a deadline and stick to it!

Write down your goals, put them somewhere you can see them, and refer to them often! Those written goals will also be useful on bad days, to remind you of why you started in the first place and to keep you from giving up when the going gets tough. You need to create actionable steps that coincide with these goals, and establish deadlines for yourself to make them happen. Of course, your daily schedule should relate back to achieving those goals. Your schedule and daily life should fill up with actionable steps and tasks that align with your goals.

If you are married or sharing your life with someone else, you'll have to take into account what success looks like for them as well. If you are married, you no longer have just your own dreams—now you're dreaming together, and that is why people typically get married in the first place. Maybe you're balancing your dreams with the dreams of your spouse. With shared dreams comes compromise, and from that struggle and strength you will learn levels of selflessness and grace you never thought possible. If you have kids together, you'll of course also have to take them into account. My husband and I have to work together constantly to achieve our own dreams, without sacrificing too much time away from the kids—or each other! My husband and I have both learned this the hard way. Of course, at times we all have to sacrifice, and though it is not always easy, the reality is that sometimes you may have to put your own dreams to the side. But I want you to remember that there will be seasons to your life. There might be times when it seems like your spouse's career is the priority, and other times when there is more room for you to follow your dreams. Or perhaps, is there a way to find space for you both to follow your dreams? I happen to think so. Through it all, keep your shared values at the forefront.

There are certain things that I am just not willing to sacrifice. You probably have some of these things in your life as well—deal breakers, so to speak, lines you're not willing to cross, sacrifices you deem too steep to justify no matter the payoff. There are pros and cons to every decision that you make and you must weigh those often. For me, being an entrepreneur and being in control of my destiny, both financially and time-wise, is very important. These are two of the most, if not the most, important factors that led me to the decision that being a business owner was the path for me. After all, I do like a challenge. But on the flip side of that coin, being an entrepreneur means risk. It means I get out of my job what I put into it, and it also means if something fails, it is because of my own efforts and actions. Another con is that sometimes on weekends, on vacation, or during family time, problems have to be addressed. But while that might seem too high a price to others, it's quite the contrary for me. Having control and responsibility is one of the things that makes me tick and inspires me, but rest assured it is not always easy. This is where knowing yourself comes into play; these are the kinds of things you need to know about yourself. What are your strengths, what are your weaknesses, and what path will lead you to the most success when defining your goals?

You should set goals for all aspects of your life. Financial, professional, spiritual, travel, personal, health, family, business—the list can be endless. If you are working to better achieve something in your life, you should create a SMART goal to go with it. Action steps accompany goals in order to make them happen. Goals also make you look at the bigger picture to make sure you have all the data you need to make them realistic. Let's look at a few examples of weak goals to see how we can make them SMART and apply some action steps to each one on the following pages.

PROFESSIONAL **GOAL**

KATIE'S WEAK GOAL: To become a photographer.

To make this SMART, we would need to look at Katie's financial goals and current situation in order to forecast a date to make the goal time-based. Once we know this information we can then create a SMART goal.

KATIE'S SMART GOAL: To be a full-time wedding photographer by 1/1 of next year, making $2,000 a month.

ACCOUNTABILITY PARTNER(S): Mr. Sorenson (mentor)

ACTION STEPS

- [x] Focus on branding and invest in a new website and logo
  DUE DATE 1 / 17 / 17

- [x] Create a marketing plan. Allocate 10 percent of projected income to marketing plan to discern the best ROI.
  DUE DATE 2 / 21 / 17

- [x] Book five weddings at rate of $2,500
  DUE DATE 8 / 21 / 17

- [x] Go part time with my current position in order to allocate time to marketing and networking to grow my business.
  DUE DATE 10 / 16 / 17

☑ COMPLETED! DATE 12 / 15 / 17

HEALTH **GOAL**

REBECCA'S WEAK GOAL: *Lose some weight in order to be healthier.*

REBECCA'S SMART GOAL: *Lose five pounds in three months by increasing exercise and eliminating processed foods and artificial sugar.*

ACCOUNTABILITY PARTNER(S): *Ashley (neighbor)*

ACTION STEPS

☑ *Join a gym and either sign up for personal training or decide which classes to attend.*   DUE DATE   4 / 1 / 17

☑ *Clean out pantry and organize it. Make a list of groceries needed to stick to new meal plan.*   DUE DATE   4 / 10 / 17

☑ *Establish an accountability partner and check in with progress every 30 days.*   DUE DATE   4 / 15 / 17

☑ *Allocate time in schedule to prep snacks and meals in order to stick to clean eating*   DUE DATE   4 / 7 / 17

☑ COMPLETED!   DATE   6 / 12 / 17

Ahead of scheduled goal!!!

FINANCIAL **GOAL**

JOHN'S WEAK GOAL: *Don't be in so much debt.*

JOHN'S SMART GOAL: *Pay off student loans within two years.*

ACCOUNTABILITY PARTNER(S): *Laura (wife)*

ACTION STEPS

☑ *Calculate how much needs to be paid on loan monthly in order to*

pay off loan in 24 months. DUE DATE *9 / 15 / 17*

☑ *Create a monthly budget with my current income and assess*

how my money is being distributed. DUE DATE *10 / 1 / 17*

☑ *See that I am spending $800 a month on groceries/eating out, and focus on meal prep in order*

to have more discretionary income to allocate to loan payments. DUE DATE *10 / 15 / 17*

☑ *Check in quarterly to see if there are any ways to make more income*

by advancing my career or picking up more responsibility. DUE DATE *11 / 1 / 17*

☑ COMPLETED! *In exactly 24 months!!*

These are just a few examples that will help you to see how you should be creating goals for your own life. Goals can sometimes also be overwhelming, and if they are, you should start breaking them down into mini-goals. Make the accomplishments and action steps as small as possible. Small steps add up to big accomplishments. If you have a small business you should create yearly, quarterly, and monthly goals, and ways to assess them with benchmarks. You were made to do incredible things and you should clearly define what success looks like to you and set SMART goals for all aspects of your life. Once you have a vision and a plan, you can do anything.

Goals should be revisited often—not just once a year. Goals are something we learn about while in elementary school, and somewhere along the way we lose the goal mentality or forget to take the time to write them down, which leads to not taking actionable steps. You must keep goals simple and SMART in order to set yourself up to succeed. You are designed to do something amazing and to be the best version of yourself, and this starts with creating those goals that govern your life. Today, right now, on the following pages, we are going to clearly define success for your life and goals to get you there.

IN BROAD TERMS WHAT IS SUCCESS TO YOU?

_____

_____

_____

_____

PROFESSIONAL SUCCESS

_____

_____

_____

PERSONAL SUCCESS

_____

_____

_____

CREATE GOALS FOR ALL ASPECTS OF YOUR LIFE

(To create more SMART goals, go to www.StartBalancing.com/downloads for a free download.)

GOAL #1

GOAL DUE DATE   /   /

_____

_____

_____

_____

ACCOUNTABILITY PARTNER(S):

ACTION STEPS

☐ _____ DUE DATE   /   /

☐ _____ DUE DATE   /   /

☐ _____ DUE DATE   /   /

☐ _____ DUE DATE   /   /

☐ _____ DUE DATE   /   /

☐ COMPLETED!   DATE   /   /

GOAL #2

GOAL DUE DATE   /   /

_____

_____

_____

_____

ACCOUNTABILITY PARTNER(S): ....

ACTION STEPS

☐ _____ DUE DATE   /   /

☐ _____ DUE DATE   /   /

☐ _____ DUE DATE   /   /

☐ _____ DUE DATE   /   /

☐ _____ DUE DATE   /   /

☐ COMPLETED!   DATE   /   /

GOAL #3

GOAL DUE DATE　　/　　/

_____

_____

_____

_____

ACCOUNTABILITY PARTNER(S):

▨ ACTION STEPS

☐ _____ DUE DATE　/　/

☐ _____ DUE DATE　/　/

☐ _____ DUE DATE　/　/

☐ _____ DUE DATE　/　/

☐ _____ DUE DATE　/　/

☐ COMPLETED!　DATE　/　/

THREE

BE ACCOUNTABLE

BUILD A TRIBE

TO HOLD YOU

ACCOUNTABLE.

—KRISTY DICKERSON

Once you've defined and written down your goals, you must now share your goals with others so that someone can hold you accountable. You then need time scheduled with those people to assess your progress on your goals and determine if you are on track or if anything needs to be altered. I have found two of the most powerful ways to make goals attainable is to write them down and to share them. As humans, we are designed not to push ourselves in times of doubt. Your accountability partner or your tribe needs to push you when you don't think you can. This may sound minor but it is one of the most important steps in giving you that push and maintaining a strong focus. We often say, "This year I want to do X"—but then we don't follow through or we lose our way. Checking in and keeping yourself accountable to your goal will help you to feel accomplished and successful. We are not always capable of pushing ourselves and seeing our full potential. Everyone needs to have individuals who hold them accountable in various areas of their life. We need to establish people in our lives who will make us do what we say we are going to do.

Sometimes life gets busy, we become lazy, or priorities start shifting when they shouldn't, and these individuals are here to keep us in line. Typically, our support systems are made up of our closest friends, family, people at work, or even coaches or mentors. From a young age, we have had individuals hold us accountable, right? Parents at home, teachers in the classroom, coaches on the court, and even our friends, but as soon as we become adults we are expected to be able to push ourselves on our own, 100 percent of the time; no one talks about accountability partners. "Adulting" is not easy, and I think no matter our age we must have people who hold us to a higher standard than we hold ourselves. We cannot always see our potential or even our faults. An accountability partner can be someone you pay or not. I am going to go over some key areas where you should establish someone to hold you accountable when doubt seeps in or a clear path is no longer visible. It could be the same person for all or a different one for each area, or it could be a group of people. You need to have someone holding you accountable for any goal you are pursing to better your life, in order to make that goal happen.

PHYSICAL. Is one of your goals to eat cleaner or exercise more? You can do group exercise, join in a challenge group, or join a friend or your spouse to get healthier together. If you are someone who is competitive, challenge groups or group exercise could be a great option for you. You can also get a personal trainer to hold you accountable and to teach you how to properly condition your body. Typically, when you are paying someone at the gym to train you and you have a certain time to meet them, you don't miss your workouts. You can also hire a nutritionist to teach you cleaner ways of eating. They generally want you to write down everything you eat or drink. When you have to share that food log with someone else, you are more likely to be self-aware about what you are eating. Living a healthier life is an important goal for a lot of individuals and we tend to do better when we learn good habits and check in with individuals on a regular basis, constantly pushing us to lead our healthiest lives.

FINANCIAL. Only about 20 percent of Americans are free from debt.[3] 44.2 million Americans had student loan debt in the fourth quarter of 2016, totaling 1.44 trillion dollars.[4] Financials will be addressed in an upcoming chapter, but the point here is to assign someone to hold you accountable for your spending, budgeting, and allocation of your financial resources. I think that, in this case, there should be a couple people involved. Do you sit down every month and make a budget? Do you assess your overall financial goals annually and look at where you will be spending your income and how much you plan to allocate to savings? Are you saving for a big purchase? Do you know exactly how much is needed for that big purchase and where exactly you will be getting the funds for it and when? Do you know how much you have to spend on groceries and food, or what your discretionary income is for the month? If you just read all that and thought to yourself, *well, I need to do more of all these things*, this is what an accountability partner does. If you are married, your spouse should be a part of this. If you are just graduating from college or even high school, get guidance from a parent or family friend who seems to be strong in this area. In any scenario, a professional financial advisor can help you set up a plan to get out of debt, make those big purchases, and set yourself up for retirement. A 2016 study by the Insured Retirement Institute revealed that only 55 percent of baby boomers had retirement savings. That is to say, 45 percent of those surveyed had *no retirement savings at all.*[5] This is a scary number and what I want for you is a plan in place so you can retire, and so your financials don't cause stress in your life, your relationships, or become a topic that your children have to deal with when you are older. We all know we are supposed to take the time to plan financials but as life gets busy and wants and needs come our way, it is really easy to turn to plastic or other means to make ends meet— and I don't want that for you.

PROFESSIONAL. A business or life coach can change the course of your career. We've talked about strengths and weaknesses, but a lot of times we are still blind to the possibilities that we are capable of. For me personally, it has been life-changing to work in a team environment. We share our goals and aspirations and when we want to quit we can't. We tend to be okay with letting ourselves down, but we don't want to let others down. If you are a solo entrepreneur or even a working professional, find someone to be your coach. Talk about what your goals are for the year. What do you want to do to advance your training, your career, or your business goals moving forward? A business coach is also experienced and typically very knowledgeable in making big decisions and can speed up the time it takes to achieve a goal by giving you a clear path with set expectations.

PERSONAL. The most important person you should make sure you are treating well and is happy is you. If you are not taking care of yourself, it is harder to take care of others. It is important that you have someone to talk with about problems, goals, and life in general, who can help you muddle through life. This can be a neutral third party or a counselor. I see a counselor on a regular basis, even though our society is wired to think you only see a counselor when you have problems. I think it is important to constantly maintain your emotional and mental state and talk about your dreams and problems with someone. There must be maintenance so that life-altering issues don't arise. This doesn't have to be someone you pay, but could be an advisor or elder that you respect, who helps you to be the best version of yourself to maintain healthy relationships with yourself and others.

SPIRITUAL. This can mean different things to different people, but you should have a sense of peace about your life and your purpose. Involve yourself in small groups, churches, or organizations that support your beliefs. For some, spirituality may be practicing yoga and being in touch with themselves. This is often a goal for individuals, but without someone to remain accountable to, it can get sacrificed. Spiritual accountability and focus will give our lives meaning and purpose.

An important part of this process is discussing with your accountability partners what is effective in motivating you. We all respond differently to criticism or feedback. Are you someone who appreciates hearing it straight, getting the brutally honest truth? Or are you someone who needs a lot of positivity and prefers to hear positive feedback to keep you moving forward? Are you a combination of both?

Set due dates and a schedule for checking in. Does your accountability partner need to encourage you daily, or will that feel overwhelming? This is an important aspect to consider so your partner can be as effective as possible in holding you accountable to your goals.

We all need to be held accountable in order to push ourselves. When establishing accountability partners for different aspects of your life, it is important to understand that this is not a one-time thing, but rather an ongoing practice of checking in and pushing each other forward. I believe that we must always have someone pouring into us and we should also be pouring into others. Discuss your life goals and ambitions with your accountability partners so they can hold you accountable and help you achieve success. We are our own worst critics and it is paramount that we have others pushing us, calling us out, and cheering us on, in order to live our lives to the fullest.

MY **ACCOUNTABILITY PARTNERS. . .**

PHYSICAL
_____

FINANCIAL
_____

PROFESSIONAL
_____

PERSONAL
_____

SPIRITUAL
_____

OTHER:
_____

OTHER:
_____

THE ONLY PERSON
YOU ARE DESTINED
TO BECOME
IS THE PERSON
YOU DECIDE
TO BE.

—RALPH WALDO EMERSON

#STARTBALANCING

FOUR

GET ORGANIZED

Organization is paramount to every other topic in this book and it is one I happen to love! This might be a battle and not a strong suit of yours. You have to organize your goals, your path, your plan of action, and virtually everything in your personal and/or business life in order to be the most productive and efficient version of yourself. Organization is how everything can work seamlessly together, and we will look at how to organize food, meal planning and prepping, clothes, workspace, miscellaneous spaces, cleaning schedules, financials, photos, digital documents, and legal and life planning. If you are not organized, you cannot get as much done. Period. If you are not organized, you will be thinking constantly about unfinished projects and wanting to get them done; lack of organization can weigh you down. Completion of projects and having organized spaces is freeing—it helps you think better and focus on bigger, more meaningful priorities. This chapter will conclude with a list of things you should get organized so you can start getting things done now.

All other aspects of this book lean on this topic. You have to be organized when it comes to your goals, your path, your plan of action, and virtually everything. Are you thinking, *I guess I'm in trouble*? This is something you can learn, or you can lean on someone for accountability. This is not a chapter you can skip over—in order to effectively balance your worlds, this is an area we are going to take a good look at and work on.

Organization gives you the ability to work efficiently, saving you money, frustration, and time. From running a fluid household to maintaining a professional life at peak productivity, being properly organized will get you there. I am going to break down the major components of getting organized so you can assess your home (and/or business) to see if there are some things you need to get organized.

What we are going to be aiming for in this chapter is a minimalistic approach, clearing out clutter, and assessing what you actually *need* and *love*. The more organized the spaces are in your home and/or office, the bigger you are able to think. If you have lingering tasks that need your attention, you will constantly be thinking about those tasks until they are completed. "Stuff" will bog you down; I myself have to constantly clean and organize different areas of my life. I couldn't find the words to write this book until I was at a point in my business and life where I felt organized. An independent study done by Brother states that on average 76 working hours per employee are lost annually because of disorganization in the workplace (which may include looking for items around the office or files on the computer).[6] If this is true for the workplace, imagine how many hours are lost at home while trying to get tasks completed. I am going to go over some of the areas you can work on and give you tips and tricks on how to start approaching your life in a more organized fashion. While organizing, decide what you need to keep, what you can donate or sell, and what you can toss. For anything you keep, is there a better way to keep it organized?

WORKSPACE. Coffee nook, desk at your office, table in your kitchen, home office, corner of a couch—wherever you go to think, plan, or work should be a space that is free of clutter and inspiring. This could be inside or outside the home, or both. I didn't always have the luxury of a dedicated office space in my home and sometimes my office consisted of a corner of my couch with a cup of coffee and the sound of a baby monitor crackling beside me. If you do not currently have a space, try to create one. If you do have a space, is it organized? Is it a space that you are excited to sit down in and that inspires you to work? Is there a pile of papers sitting on the desk? Are they papers that need to be filed away or that need your attention? Is there a system for processing items and workflows in place so you don't create a bigger mess? Creating an organized workspace that you love is often overlooked, but I think it is so important, especially if you work from home. Sometimes it is hard to separate the responsibilities of being at home and what you need to get done professionally—having a space to separate the two helps. This applies whether you are running a household, working from home, or running a business. In order to be productive you have to be organized. If you do not have a clean workspace, you have to get it clean. Start going through the piles of documents on your desk and sorting them by those that are already paid and need to be filed, items to shred, and items to pay or respond to. If you haven't already, get a filing cabinet or folders and sort any documents that you need to save. I have a designated spot for each company I own. Each company has a file for legal and corporate documents, expenses, bank statements, and, depending on the company's needs, payouts, employees, and so on. You could also go digital, scan the items, and set up a system for organization on your computer as well. I am going to touch on digital organization in a moment.

From a personal perspective, you should have a file for insurance, investments, house mortgage/deed, home improvements, cars, medical files for each family member, and any revolving loans or debt. I also keep a copy of anything really important in a safe or safety deposit box. Some of this may be automated so you won't need to keep a physical record of it. Once you get everything organized and sorted, you then need to set up a workflow and system to maintain that organization. On my desk I have files to sort documents as I get them: "pending," "to pay," and "to file." It is not efficient to pay every bill as it arrives; rather, designate a place for bills and have set days every month when you pay and organize them.

From a personal perspective, I have a desk in my home with some folders that I use to organize items I want to keep—for instance, school art or work. My kids bring home all sorts of arts, crafts, and homework. When I get it, I filter through for any items that are personal or that really show their current capabilities. I place that work in a file that has their name on it and discard the rest. Then at the end of every year, I scan that artwork and make it into a small book so that we can look back and enjoy it in a non-cluttered way.

The less you have on the desk, the better. If it is not something that you need in order to get things done or for inspiration, then find another place for it. For some reason or another, my desk collects all sorts of pens, pencils, markers, and other random things. I go through these items on occasion and get rid of what I don't use; this keeps clutter off my desk. A cluttered desk is a cluttered mind. The more positive, clean, and organized your workspace is, the more you can get done and the bigger you can dream.

HOME. Now that we've addressed where you will be dreaming up your big ideas and getting things done, let's assess where you live. Your home might be a bedroom, a dorm room, an apartment, or an entire house. I would start with the room that you frequent the most. Make a list, in priority order, of all the rooms in your home and go through them all, even if you think, *that room is fine.*

- What do you need in the room?
- Is there anything you can sell or donate?
- Is there anything that doesn't fit or you will never use again?
- Do you need to purchase bins or organizational tools to complete projects?
- What items make you feel joyful, energized, calm, fulfilled, nostalgic, etc.?

Go through drawers and cabinets assessing whether you have duplicates or clutter filling up your space. Going room by room, make a list of further things that need organizing or need your attention. Take it one room at a time and knock it out! Remember to make a list of any donations so you can use them on your tax return!

FOOD. It is a necessity of life and it is something that I am always thinking about. In our fast-paced world, society caters easy solutions to fill this gap, but they are not always the healthiest options, nor are they the most economical. I am going to touch on health in a later chapter, but here I want to focus on how you organize your food. First you need to clean out, straighten, and declutter your pantry, from spices to dry goods. Once you know what you have you can build a weekly dinner menu and develop a grocery list to go along with it. If I go to the grocery store without a plan, I come home with so many things that I don't need and then I am off my budget and creating clutter. I am an impulse buyer and if I see something new on an endcap I think I need to have it—this is a weakness of mine! You know all those marketing campaigns that companies spend tens of thousands of dollars on? I am their ideal target. Going in with a plan and knowing exactly what you need saves you money and time, and you won't have to make multiple trips to the store throughout the week.

If you don't know what you are having for dinner, lunch, or snacks, this is something that is in the back of your mind and can take away your focus and productivity throughout the day. Having this already mapped out at the beginning of the week and prepping as much as possible helps to save money, helps to save time, and allows you to make healthier choices. Prepping meals is a great way to save time. Sundays are my prep days and I try to cook, sort, and pack as many meals as possible to save time throughout the week. I drink green smoothies every morning and I make them on Sundays so that throughout the week I just pull one out of the freezer at night and it is ready for me in the morning. Some Sundays I am unable to prep meals, so I come up with a different time and plan so that the prep is taken care of for the week. Organizing the food in your pantry and in your fridge, and planning your meals will save you so much time and avoid unnecessary waste of money and food.

CLOTHES. Minimalism is a new approach that I have been taking toward clothing. If you haven't cleaned out or organized your closet in a while, it is time. I try to do it twice a year, and if I didn't wear something over that last season it is probably time for it to go. I organize my clothes by colors and seasons and turn my hangers backwards so that I can see what I am wearing and what I am not. Once an item has been worn, I put its hanger back the correct way. Cleaning out my closet is not an easy task for me because, for some reason, I develop a personal relationship with my clothes. It helps to have a friend or someone else go through your closet with you. I was hanging on to a pair of jeans because I had paid a lot of money for them. They were too big, and keeping them was like encouraging myself to gain that weight back. You also need to go through your shoes. I had seven pairs of black heels in my closet—and I rarely wear black heels. When I do, I pick the same ones every time. So why do I have seven? I wear roughly 20 percent of the clothes that I own and I think this is true for a lot of people.

Typically, I wear the most recent items I've purchased and forget about a lot of great pieces that I love but haven't worn recently. Try laying out clothes for yourself (and your kids) before the week starts. Could you create a system for bringing in new clothes? If you purchase a new piece, can you part with one you are no longer wearing? This saves a lot of time when you are in a hurry to get out the door. I am usually in a hurry to get everywhere so I need to save time wherever I can. Once you have tackled your closet, it is also important to organize and clean out your children's closets if you have kids. My kids are growing so I have to do this literally every season so that I can assess what they have and what they need. Sell or get rid of things you can no longer use!

Once you take out all the things you no longer like, that don't fit, or that you don't need, organize the rest by season, by type, and if you want to get really fancy, by color. The goal is to establish a good system to organize your clothes so that when you need them you can easily locate them. For my kids, I have found that if I just stack T-shirts the traditional way, they will always wear the T-shirt on top of the stack in the drawer. Instead, I fold the T-shirts and then roll them up so that the kids can see all their shirts.

Styles change, and your own personal style will change! Cleaning out my closet is not an easy task for me but I swear you will be able to think so much more clearly if you know what you have and what you need! Organization also gives you the ability to fill in any gaps in your wardrobe that you might need to complete outfits.

CLEANING/MAINTENANCE. This book is not just for parents, but if you have kids cleaning is a daily occurrence. There are daily tasks that have to get done in and around the home and there are things that can be handled on a weekly or bimonthy basis. There are also things that you have to do quarterly and even annually. Sometimes "adulting" just isn't fun, but it is a part of life. Daily cleaning includes taking out trash, wiping counters, doing dishes, sweeping, and doing laundry; weekly/bimonthy is cleaning bathrooms, dusting, mopping, and changing bed sheets. Every quarter or six months you also have tasks such as changing air filters, water filters, and cleaning outside windows and gutters. You need to organize how all these tasks will get done, either by delegating, outsourcing, or scheduling time out for yourself. Lawn care also falls under cleaning and maintenance. If you own your home there are also things around your house that you will need to maintain. Planting flowers, staining wood, painting, changing light bulbs—the list could go on and on.

I've just been talking about your home, but if you have a car, this will have to be taken into account as well. Clean it regularly and make sure you are keeping up with the routine maintenance. Create a system with lists and reminders in order to keep up with it all. Your home and car are assets and doing the proper cleaning and maintenance helps you to maintain the value of your asset.

FINANCIALS. Be organized with your money. I can't even begin to express the importance of setting up a system to keep this organized, to track, and to take care of financial tasks. Is there someone in your family who is better at this than you? If so, work together with them. A budget needs to be set for every household so that you can track spending and allocate resources to things you want to do, future assets, and for savings. If you are married and neither you nor your spouse is good at this, talk to a financial advisor. If you are single, having someone look at your financial dreams and creating a plan for monetary goals is crucial in order to set SMART goals. Financial knowledge is one of the most important life tools but for some reason it is not taught in our school system or to our youth. We typically are not taught how to "adult"—we just learn it through trial and error. For that reason, debt can start at an early age and it can become a cumbersome problem if you don't properly set up a plan to break free.

Once you have SMART financial goals in place, set up a workflow in order to maintain the system. I pay bills twice a month. That doesn't necessarily work for everyone, but establishing a day or two every month to pay bills is important. Having an organized filing system for this is important as well. Many of my personal bills are paid through automated withdrawals, but my business bills, which are not automated, need to be recorded, and I always use the filing system I created for my workspace. It is important to make sure you have financials properly filed and allocated. Find a trusted advisor to help with this if it is not your strong point, or even if it is, just so you have someone to hold you accountable. Financials need to be assessed and taken care of monthly with a clear vision of the whole year always in sight. For my home expenses, a monthly review is fine, but for my small business establishing benchmarks and assessing daily is often vital in order to make marketing, ordering, and other business decisions.

From a personal perspective, setting preliminary budgets and forecasts will help you decide what you will do for that month, quarter, and year. Without creating a forecast of income and expenses, how will you know where you can vacation, or when you can pay off your car or buy a home? You won't know what childcare you can afford, or how much you can allocate to groceries, or how much discretionary income you will have. You won't know when will be a good time to buy a house or what the budget for that house should be.

From a business perspective, how do you know when you can afford to make that next investment, how much to allocate to marketing funds, when you will be able to start paying yourself, or when you will be able to hire someone? And that's just from the expense perspective. What about inventory projections? How will you know how much inventory to order and what resources to put into place without projecting your income and marketing, and allocating cost funds? The list could go on and on. If you run a small business, knowing and understanding your numbers is very important. Again, if this is not a strong point of yours, partner with someone or outsource this because, although you don't have to be the one doing it, you do need to be able to interpret and understand all aspects of your business in order to make decisions.

I say no to debt. Remember, debt is also different from financial leverage. Debt to me is when you take out money to buy something without a specific reason or schedule to pay it back. Financial leverage is when you borrow someone else's money with a specific plan and schedule to pay it back. You don't want any kind of "debt." *Ever.* And in the spirit of full disclosure I will say that in the past I have had debt. I (we) have made bad/uneducated decisions and lost money, or worse yet, we wasted money. Would anyone else want to go back and change a financial decision they made or something that they bought? I think so. When you have debt, someone else controls your actions and decisions, and you owe them.

There are a lot of financial advisors who say no to credit cards, and if your problem is with cards this may be a good idea. This goes back to knowing yourself. If you know that money management is a weakness and cards are an enabler, then yes, remove that temptation. Credit cards, if you are able to manage them, can be a great thing; I have gone on many trips using credit card points. For these credit card companies, it is a business and the individuals who don't pay their bills and get charged interest are offsetting those partnership costs where points are rewarded. You want to be the one benefiting from rewards points and not the one paying interest on a balance. Another benefit of using cards is that everything can sync and automate in your systems so that you can track your spending to know where your money is going, saving you time as well. I also want to note that if you are a business owner, it is important to maintain clear books, with separate bank accounts and credit cards that all have a clear paper trail.

My husband and I live by a simple principle for our personal financials: if we cannot pay cash for it, we don't buy it. This isn't something we've always done. Thinking back over the last decade, there have been so many resources wasted. What I would tell my younger self is to save, save, save. Make smart financial decisions in order to spend your hard-earned money on memories that you plan to make or on sound financial investments.

Debt is something that controls you instead of you controlling it, and your life is something you should be in complete control of. As soon as you assume debt, you have a commitment to someone other than yourself. Wouldn't it be awesome to only have commitments to yourself? You can do this! I do realize it is harder to do with bigger assets like a house, and with a house you can also get tax write-offs. Ask yourself an important question before you buy something: if you were to lose your primary source of income, could you still pay for it? If you just took a big gulp, then you might want to consider how you can make some small changes that will make a big impact.

Establish a "rainy day account." This is something we are told to do from a young age. I do agree but I think another thing that you need to do, which is not stressed enough, is diversify your investments. In 2007, the U.S. housing market crumbled and our stock market and economy soon followed. Such economic scenarios are destined to happen, and it is important that you set yourself up to ride those storms. Life will happen and unexpected expenses that were not accounted for will come your way. The goal here is to be prepared for them. I am not a financial advisor, and don't advise anyone on specifics, but I am someone who knows the importance of having a plan and proper allocation of your funds to give you freedom!

Giving is something I think we all need to do more of. It is a selfless act and it is something I am constantly working to do more of. There are many ways that you can give and although I am outlining this in the financial section, there are other resources that you can give. You might think, *I can't give until I get myself out of debt.* But you would be surprised, with a plan in place and by tracking your spending, what opportunities might become available. I think that giving grounds us, gives us purpose, and reminds us how well-off we are. No matter how small individual donations may be, they add up to big things.

This section is hard for a lot of people to cover. "Money problems" and financial stress can cause health issues and can break up marriages. What I want for you in this section is to get your money organized and to put a plan in place. There are many great books and resources that can help you to understand budgeting better. Getting out of debt takes time but my hope is that you will master your financials so they are no longer a burden.

PERSONAL AUDIT. Self-care is something we also need to make sure we are taking into account. We only have one body, and often we don't take care of it properly. If we don't take care of our bodies and maintain them, we are selling ourselves short. Make sure you have a primary care physician and a dentist, both of whom you like and trust. If you do not, do some research and find recommendations for good doctors. Make sure you are attending your checkups on a regular basis. Staying organized with respect to your health and personal well-being is crucial not only for achieving success, but for living a healthy life.

PHOTOS/VIDEOS. We live in a world of Instagram, iPhone photos, and DSLRs. Often, the memories we capture don't get organized. The photos are your history (and your kids' history) and it is important to make sure you properly store, back up, and print them in a way that can be enjoyed by family and friends. There are many different methods for doing this but I am going to share what works for me. After shooting pictures, import them to a program that allows you to rename your images with a new filename. I always use YearMonthDayCustomSeq but it can be anything, as long as you establish as a system and use it! For example, if I take pictures on a trip to Disney World, the file names would look like this: 20170724Disney001. Organize all the events together into a folder for the year. By creating an organized system, you can easily locate images when needed. You also need to make sure to have a cloud service to back up those images so your files will be safe even if the hard drive fails or any natural disaster occurs.

Printing and organizing your photos is so important in order to archive them for your family and for you and others to enjoy. It is also another method of backing up and preserving images. I get our family pictures done annually and those photos are in an album, vacations typically end up having an album of their own, and then I do one album that is the year in review. I typically do all of my photo books once a year, or immediately after a big trip or event. Place the albums somewhere family and friends can enjoy. The important thing here is to create a workflow for getting your images from your camera (or phone) to a finished product, while also creating a method to archive your images in an organized way.

This also goes for videos or footage you are shooting. If you are taking videos, make sure you edit and cut out any footage you don't need and get the videos to a finished state so you can watch and enjoy. Just like the photos, organize them into folders and rename the videos so that you can archive them and be able to locate and enjoy them for years to come. Videos also take up a lot of hard drive space so it is important to cull and edit in order to optimize your storage.

Is this something you really struggle with? Is it because technology scares you and you're not sure of the right software? There are classes and online resources to help, or you can connect with a friend who is really good at this to help show you the way. More pictures and videos than ever are being taken, but how many of those pictures are going to be passed down to future generations? I want you to be able to establish workflows for your memories so that for years to come, you and your loved ones will be able to enjoy the life that you lived.

DIGITAL DOCUMENTS. Organizing your files, documents, and images digitally allows you to archive and sort your documents. Cloud services are the best way to organize and sort documents, in my opinion. I have a desktop, laptop, and phone, and I keep my documents stored on a cloud platform, allowing me to access my files at any time, from any device. Organization of documents is also important so you don't waste time looking for files. Create separate folders for companies, projects, or personal needs. For each of these folders, create a Resource folder where you can place important information or things you have to access often. Label that folder with an asterisk so it will always show up first (*Resources). Then organize the rest of your folders by name for quick referencing. For instance, in the resource folder for my business, I include my logo, current headshot, signed version of W9 with EIN number so that I can easily and quickly find them. As life happens, folders and files can become disorganized; scheduling time to organize and audit your files to ensure they are properly allocated is key. You don't want to waste your time searching for files or trying to remember where things are. When saving files, use a system for anything requiring edits. For instance, when I'm working on a document it would be called NAMEV1, then V2, and then once it is in its final state it no longer has a version number. Remember to delete any duplicates or old versions of documents. You also need to make sure your photos and all digital documents are backed up via a cloud service and occasionally do audits to make sure your files are safe. I have had a computer crash and if I had not properly backed up my documents, it could have been devastating. Make sure you organize your computer and set times to recheck your organization system as life gets busy, so you can always keep a "clean house."

COMMUNICATION. You must be organized in how you communicate with others. Set up systems, workflows, and protocols for all forms of communication. This includes phones, tablets, and laptops, and it means making sure that your voicemail, iMessages, and your emails are all properly synced and sorted. Emails is a big one, as it is one of the most common forms of communication we use, and it is important that you keep it organized by auditing it often. If you have accounts set up with tons of unread messages (you know who you are) get them organized. It is also a good idea to have different emails for different functions. I have an email for personal endeavors, an email for STARTplanner, and also an email for speaking engagements. Within our company, all individuals have emails; in addition we have accounts set up for specific needs such as PR or Customer Service. Create folders within each of your accounts so you can file away old emails as you sort through them. Delete and unsubscribe from any unnecessary subscriptions. Your email should be something you can reference for information and a way to communicate to get things done. In order to do this, you must be organized and have a system for it.

If you don't need an email, trash it. If this is something you are way behind on, schedule time to do it and break it up into chunks of time. Once done, just stick to the system moving forward so your inbox stays organized!

LEGAL. This is the part no one wants to think about or do, but it is something that needs to be done, especially if you have a family. From a legal standpoint you always need to make sure you separate your business endeavors from your personal assets. From a business perspective, if something happens to you, how will the business dissolve? Does someone in your family need life insurance in case the unthinkable happens to one of the primary caregivers? Do you have retirement accounts set up? Do you have a will in place for yourself? If you have kids this is a step you do not want to miss. Sometimes these are hard questions to answer but they are very important. Make sure you communicate to the executor of your will how and where to get important documents. Once a year, create or reorganize a file that has everything important together in a secure place: will, insurance policies, bank account numbers, and so on. Ask yourself: if something happened to you or your spouse would the other partner know exactly what to do and be financially secure?

Are your personal assets covered under insurance policies? Once a year, take pictures or even a video of all major personal assets. Create a folder that stores and organizes documentation of assets (photos, video, receipts for major purchases) and assess it on a yearly basis—and of course make sure it is backed up via a cloud service. These are things we always push to the back of our minds, but are crucial to get done in the event the unthinkable does happen.

◇ ◇ ◇

If you are not organized, you will be less productive. You'll waste time searching for things if you haven't set up systems. If there are areas in your life that need to be organized, they are always in the back of your mind as something you know you need to do, weighing you down emotionally. Organization gives you control of your thoughts and is the baseline for all your systems. If you are saying to yourself, *Yes, this is me*, create a list, schedule it out, find someone to help and/or hold you accountable, and get organized! If you are already an organized individual, kudos to you. Keep it up! Organization is something that won't happen overnight, so it is important to make a list, prioritize, and start making things happen!

Not only will you be more productive if your life is organized, you will save money from unnecessary spending in the process. Start compiling a list of everything you want to organize and declutter in your home or office, and allocate time to it. Living a more minimalistic lifestyle will be freeing, will set you up to succeed with systems running efficiently, and will also give you more discretionary income to invest in experiences or other things that you want to allocate money to.

If you know organization is a weakness of yours or there are just some lingering areas that need your attention, we are going to change that. At the end of the chapter is a worksheet that will start you off in the right direction, and there is an accompanying PDF if you want to dive in deeper. Don't look at everything; just start taking it piece by piece. Remember, small victories add up to big things! You got this!

FOR EVERY MINUTE SPENT
IN ORGANIZING,
AN HOUR IS EARNED.

—BENJAMIN FRANKLIN

#STARTBALANCING

GET YOURSELF **ORGANIZED!**

Below are the key areas that were outlined in the chapter to get organized. Establish a due date for them all, have someone hold you accountable, and get busy! To help you navigate this process, I have created a more in-depth download for you to use as a tool to clearly establish the specific action items within each area that you need to declutter. Remember, small accomplishments add up to big victories.

Grab the PDF here: www.**Start**Balancing.com/downloads

☐ **WORKSPACE**

☐ **HOME**

☐ **FOOD**

☐ **CLOTHES**

☐ **CLEANING/MAINTENANCE**

☐ **FINANCIALS**

☐ **PERSONAL AUDIT**

☐ **PHOTOS/VIDEOS**

☐ **DIGITAL DOCUMENTS**

☐ **COMMUNICATION**

☐ **LEGAL**

THINGS IN MY LIFE TO ORGANIZE

☐ _____ DUE DATE / /

☐ _____ DUE DATE / /

☐ _____ DUE DATE / /

☐ _____ DUE DATE / /

☐ _____ DUE DATE / /

☐ _____ DUE DATE / /

☐ _____ DUE DATE / /

☐ _____ DUE DATE / /

☐ _____ DUE DATE / /

☐ _____ DUE DATE / /

☐ _____ DUE DATE / /

☐ _____ DUE DATE / /

FIVE

GET FOCUSED

REMEMBER
THAT IF YOU DON'T
PRIORITIZE
YOUR LIFE
SOMEONE ELSE WILL.

—GREG MCKEOWN

You know what success looks like; you know your strengths and weaknesses; and you are organized. Now you can start creating a plan and focusing in on harnessing your efforts. Creating a clear plan involves having a very clear vision of your SMART goals. This plan will most likely be revised along the way, forcing you to reassess it often. Actually, let me rephrase that: your plan *will* be revised. Things in life very rarely work out the way you plan them. However, in order to get where you are going, it is important to have a vision, create a plan, and align all the resources that you will need in order to bring your plan to fruition.

Resources are limited. Economy, availability, time, and location are all factors that affect you and your efforts. I say that the most valuable and limited resource is time. Have you ever said to yourself, *I need a clone?* Time is something we cannot get back, and how we choose to live our lives and balance our ambitions affects every aspect of our lives. Ultimately, where we decide to spend our time is what will make up our lives.

Focusing our efforts when creating a plan is how we progress in our goals when working with limited resources. If you are working on ten different things, you will only be able to progress slightly in each of the areas, and I fully believe you will be distracted by going back and forth on tasks. Instead, focus your time and allocate your efforts to your goals, keeping in mind your strengths and weaknesses. Pick one thing and give it your all. From a professional perspective, having one main focus will set the tone for that day. Whatever my focus is, it governs how I spend the first four hours of my work day. I know that I am my most productive and focused during the mornings so my afternoons are for meetings and other tasks. You never know how much time you'll have and prioritizing how you spend it is important. Time is a bankable resource that can positively affect our future success.

If you have a business, want to pursue a business, or want to advance in the corporate world, one of the best things you can do for yourself is focus your efforts. You should stand for one thing. From a branding perspective, if you are everything to everyone, this sends a mixed message. Some people believe that if you are very specific in what you do, you limit your pool of potential consumers too much, but I think it is the opposite. For instance, I was a wedding photographer for five years. If I had been a baby photographer and commercial photographer, and pursued other ventures how could I have allocated any time to grow my network? Remember, we have a limited amount of time. Where would I have invested resources to market my services? How would I have known how to brand my website when I was not entirely clear who my market would be? You guessed it—it would have been a lot harder. If you represent one "idea" or "thing," your branding, your website, your marketing, and everything else has a clear focus. You can zero in and know who that audience is, study to understand how to market to them, know where to invest your time and energy in building relationships, and this list could go on and on. When you are one exclusive "thing," you are also an expert in that field and can charge a premium for your services. If you need brain surgery, you'll go to a neurologist, not a general practitioner, right? I believe the same applies to business. Now more than ever, there is so much noise and competition in the market and you have to be able to clearly convey your value in today's competitive field. Even if you don't own a business, these same principles still apply. Knowing what you are good at, and focusing on that, makes you a valued asset.

Starting is sometimes the hardest part of a plan, and I believe that you should pick one goal to focus on in your work week. The first four hours of each day should be governed by that task alone. This should be done daily until you have completed that goal, and then you can move on to the next thing. If your goal for the month is to get organized, then you should delegate the first four hours, and assign yourself different spaces to complete organizational tasks. If your goal is to restructure the operations department within the company, the first four hours of the day should be spent focusing on tasks that relate to making that happen. If you work full time and time is of the essence, then pick one or two tasks for a weekend and wake up early so that you are able to get more done. For me, this book is a testament to all of this—I had to push other goals aside and focus on making writing a priority by dedicating the first four hours of the day to making this dream a reality. I also had to do this when the timing was right.

I am not saying that you can't focus on multiple goals in different areas of your life at the same time, but I am saying that with professional ambitions, you need to focus on one. Imagine there are four cars on a race track. Each car represents a professional goal you are trying to achieve. There are only so many hours in the day that you can drive those cars. If you are trying to drive all four at the same time and you only have four hours to do so, you will be bouncing back and forth between the different cars every hour. Instead, when you focus, you pick one car and focus all your energy and time toward that one goal for the four hours. Which car will reach the finish line first? Not only first, but which car will have a higher quality race and end product? You got it: the car that you spent the majority of your efforts moving forward and focusing on, avoiding distractions. Once you complete a goal you can move your efforts to the next. This also ensures that you are not distracted and constantly multitasking throughout the day, leaving you more productive and also resulting in a better end product.

Start by envisioning what you want, then create a plan to get you there. In a nutshell, if you are not setting goals and creating a plan to get there, you are blindly walking through life. Will you get lucky on occasion? Maybe. But you have a much greater chance of success if you know where you are going, why you are going, and how you are going to get there. Yes, even though you set a path, you will sometimes fall short, your direction will completely change, or your life circumstances will change everything. That is the beauty and the struggle of life. Sometimes it is not about just the end goal, but the journey. You cannot create a plan and expect it to execute itself. You have to be ready to do the work in order to get yourself there!

MY BIGGEST DISTRACTIONS

_____

_____

_____

WAYS TO OVERCOME DISTRACTIONS

_____

_____

_____

TOP PLACES TO FOCUS MY ATTENTION

_____

_____

_____

_____

SIX

MANAGE YOUR TIME

All the chapters thus far have addressed how you should manage your schedule by outlining your goals in order to properly *Start Balancing*. We have established that your most limited resource is time and that you need to be very selective with your time. Time is something none of us have enough of and, to be honest, we really do not even know how long we have. Think about it. If you knew you had one week left to live, how much more intentionally would that time be spent? This chapter is going to give specific tips on how to manage your schedule and, more precisely, your time. You will get tips on how to manage your calendar so you can be your most efficient and productive self, so that you can spend more time with whomever you want, doing whatever you want!

How you choose to spend your time is important. And it all goes back to knowing yourself and your goals. I have been in places in my life where I wanted to work and be a mom but felt like I was failing at both. I have also been at places in my life where I wanted to be a stay-at-home mother and realized that that left me as a mediocre mother because I wasn't being fulfilled. No one can tell you what is right or wrong for you, and you will have to figure out what you need, define success for yourself, get organized, be focused, and then manage your time appropriately.

We cannot get time back. We can always pick our professional ambitions back up, but we cannot stop our kids from growing. If you are someone whose "cup is made fuller" by working, then work. I know with every fiber of my being that having a purpose outside of the home makes me a better mother. I don't work for the money. I work for the challenge, for the responsibility, to make an impact, and I work for me. Guess what? That is okay. There are joys in having a purpose outside of the home. You might be thinking, *I am in the corporate world and my only goal in life is to be a stay-at-home mom.* That is okay—we are all designed differently and only you can decide what is the right way to spend your time. I work for myself, so I can control my own schedule, making it to the kids' games, field trips, doctors' appointments, and so on. Most days I work from a home office so that my kids can access me and I can be there if they need me. I can also choose the hours that I work. I also want to note that I have a supportive husband who helps keep our family glued together while I chase my dreams. For me, what I am doing is the best of both worlds. I am teaching my children to pursue their dreams. Don't think it is glamorous—most days it's just me in workout gear, doing the business hustle and striving to be the best mom that I can be. What I am saying here is give yourself some grace and know that you will probably go through a discovery process of realizing what you need. You might also go through phases of your life where you have to put your ambitions on hold to support your spouse or to make ends meet.

I firmly believe you should focus on quality and not quantity, both in the office and at home. Don't guilt yourself into thinking you can't do it by setting standards for yourself based on society's expectations or by setting high benchmarks for yourself. Yes, you are going to have days and moments where life's demands seem to be more than what you are capable of doing. This is normal and is part of the process. Organizing your personal and professional pursuits, taking care of yourself, and creating a schedule to allow for task completion is important. I am going to go through some tips to help you find more time in your day to be productive so that you can spend more time doing things that you enjoy with the people you love.

WAKE UP EARLY. You have heard the saying "The early bird gets the worm." When you are balancing multiple pursuits, the only way to find success is to try to stay ahead of the game. Your most limited resource is time and being very selective with your time, while not sacrificing anything, is going to be the key. My single most important piece of advice is to wake up early. Start your day ahead of everyone. I know that if I wake up two hours before everyone else, I'll get two hours of peace and quiet to get stuff done and to focus. I start my day ahead of the curve instead of behind it! If you always feel like you are drowning in work or things around the home don't seem to get done, then get up! Everyone always says to me, "I am not a morning person." Well, I didn't use to be either. I would burn the midnight oil; sleeping in was my jam. What changed? I realized that the only way I was going to balance motherhood with the pursuit of my entrepreneurial dreams was to wake up early. The first week is the hardest. Don't hit the snooze button; get up, get started, and after about 30 minutes of working, you'll realize how much you've gotten done and you will be stoked! You value your sleep? Yes, me too! Trust me, you will start to get tired early—I am usually in bed by 9:00 p.m. It's important for your health that you are getting enough sleep. When scheduling your wake-up time, make sure you are going to bed at a decent hour as well.

CREATE TO-DO LISTS. Whether you plan on paper or digitally, starting your day by creating a list of items to get done is so important. I never stop creating lists, and typically my list is 80 percent planned the night before, as this "brain dump" keeps me from lying in bed thinking about all the things that I need to get done. Prioritizing your list also helps you to tackle items in the order of importance. It gives you direction and a plan for the day. Your daily "to-dos" should align with projects and tasks that help you achieve your mini and overarching goals. Creating a list gives you a direction, so that you can get the most done even when distractions happen. . . because they will.

PRIORITIZE. This starts with being able to see and understand your top priorities and spending the first part of the day focusing on them. This changes for me depending on my monthly goals and what is happening in our business. Right now, my top priority is writing this book, so during the work week my first four hours of the day, when I am really focused, is spent writing. Prioritizing your list ensures that the most important items get tackled first.

EMAILS. Never start your day by checking emails. This is a tough one for me, because I like to be briefed on what has happened since I last checked emails. Usually, however, your emails will alter your to-do list and will end up wasting your time, when you could have been spending it completing a lot of big items that were due. Instead, start on your to-dos and wait to check your emails until after you have gotten in at least two to three hours of work. This is hard for me because I am a doer. I am type A, and typically very fast to respond, but if I answer emails as they come in throughout the day, I am not effectively using my time, nor am I probably fully answering the emails as I should be. Schedule three times to check your emails. For example, I wake up at 5:00, work for a couple hours, help get the kids off to school, work out, and I am typically back in my office by 9:00—I check emails then. I check them again around lunch and before I leave work for the day (or before I go to bed).

Emails are a great form of communication and they can save you a ton of time by freeing you up from having to be on the phone or going to in-person meetings. You have to use emails effectively, though, and not allow them to become something that takes up your time or pulls you away from other things you could be getting done. When you create a schedule, go ahead and allocate three times during the day for checking emails and stick to this plan.

ELIMINATE DISTRACTIONS. Distractions will derail your productivity. In a study from the University of California, Irvine, researchers shadowed workers on the job, studying their productivity. Gloria Mark states that after a distraction, "You have to completely shift your thinking, it takes you a while to get into it and it takes you a while to get back and remember where you were. . . . We found about 82 percent of all interrupted work is resumed on the same day. But here's the bad news—it takes an average of 23 minutes and 15 seconds to get back to the task."[7] Now imagine distractions happening over and over throughout the day. Of course there are major distractions and minor ones, but the key is to try to eliminate as many as possible. Distractions can include phones, messages, emails, social media, spouses, mailman, kids—I mean this list can go on and on.

Let's talk about some ways to try to eliminate distractions. Scheduling times and making systems for communication is one way that we can eliminate them in the work environment. Silence mode is another way. You can turn off notifications on your computers and devices if you really need to focus on a particular task. Choosing the right location to work is another way to try to eliminate distractions. My office is detached from our house above the garage, so I do have a little separation, and we also have an office and warehouse for our business. I pick which location I am going to work in depending on my tasks at hand for the day. I used to have my office in a room inside the home that was close to the family, and the kids would constantly ask me questions. The closer you are to the family (or others), the more distractions you will have. Period. "Mom can you open this drink for me?" "Honey what did we decide to do for dinner tonight?" "Can you help me figure out this customer support email?" When you are mid-thought, or on a call, or worse in a meeting, this can derail your train of thought.

The reverse is also true: it is important to eliminate work-related distractions when we are on "personal time." "Can you give Mommy one more moment to respond to this email?" While sitting at dinner you realize you forgot to send over that proposal and you have to excuse yourself from the family. While out with friends you get a work-related phone call

BEFORE ANYTHING ELSE, PREPARATION IS THE KEY TO SUCCESS.

—ALEXANDER GRAHAM BELL

#STARTBALANCING

that you answer. You don't want your loved ones to remember you being glued to your job, and you don't have to make yourself available at all times of the day. As important as it is to schedule in work time, it is important to schedule in family time and communicate this to everyone. If you are always working or distracted, and never fully focused on your work or your family, you are spreading yourself too thin and not able to fully engage wherever you currently are.

PREPARE. Being prepared for the expected and the unexpected is what will allow you to manage your schedule and better handle any situation that arises. Making lists and blueprints for tasks is key: being prepared for the kids' lunches, your lunches, dinners, social events, work meetings, and being prepared in case the unthinkable happens. You have to be prepared so that when an opportunity arises, you're ready.

BLOCK YOUR TIME. Blocking time is, in essence, designating times within a day or entire days to a specific thing. While you are doing this, group related things together. For me, this means grouping meetings on the same day, and back-to-back. Same thing for yearly doctor visits: I schedule them all in one day, back-to-back. It is much more efficient to do that while you are already out and about, as opposed to needing to take time off on various days. Allocate time for breaks, working out, and personal goals as well! Time blocking will help you prepare for your day and eliminate distractions.

On the next page you will see an example of time blocking on your schedule (■) as well as your early wake-up (■), top three priorities (■), and your self-care (■).

SAMPLE

- WAKE UP!!
6 RUN - 3 Miles

7 ▽

8 WORK

9

10

11

12 LUNCH w/ RENEE
@ Chipotle

1

2

3

4

PHONE CALLS/REGISTRATIONS

5 ▽

DINNER + CHORES

6 ↓

7 BACK-TO-SCHOOL NIGHT

8 ▽

PRIORITIZE

1 REGISTER FOR COOKING CLASS

2 SIGN UP FOR MARATHON

3 CLEAN OFF PORCH + SWEEP

♥ WORK OUT

TO DO

✓ laundry

✓ make marathon
     training schedule

✓ EMILY'S BIRTHDAY - call

✓ call mom

A M
P M

1
2
3
💧4
💧5
💧6
💧7
💧8

SAY NO. Why is this so hard to do? We want to be able to do everything and please everyone. Saying no is something you must practice, and know that it is okay to say it. If there is something that doesn't align with your goals, then you should not commit yourself to it. We only have so much time and if we constantly fill our schedules with tasks that don't help us complete our own goals, we will never achieve them. I am not suggesting that you say no to anything and everything—of course family and friends will need you—but don't make a habit of saying yes to everyone. There is a difference between saying yes to some things and overcommitting yourself. You need to say yes to yourself more and make sure you are not trying to please everyone.

OPTIMIZE YOUR WORKING ENVIRONMENT. Take a good look at your workspace to make sure it is not only organized but planned for you to do your best work. You can use smells such as essential oils to keep you focused, decorate your office with things you love and that inspire you, and if possible set up your desk next to a window to have some natural light pouring in. Optimizing your work environment also means knowing when you are at your most productive and blocking this time to focus on your main objectives for the day!

In order to manage your schedule, you must apply these tips to maximize your efficiency by organizing tasks into chunks of time. Quality time versus quantity of time is important when you are re-evaluating how you are spending your day. You are not a superhero. You don't have magic skills that allow you to be everything to everyone. You have to set yourself up to be as productive and efficient as possible by waking up early, creating a schedule and a to-do list, eliminating distractions, and most importantly, sticking to your plans. That is what will enable you to do everything you need to do. You sometimes have to say no to anything that will pull you away from work or home life and that doesn't align with your goals. You have to be in control of your schedule and dedicated to sticking with it.

Time is such a precious thing that you have to learn to manage. I dedicated this book to my Aunt Tina, who was like an older sister to me. At age 38 she went to the doctor with a sore throat, and eight months later lost her life to cancer. Cancer and other illnesses are affecting so many; I am sure you have someone in your life who is going through a similar battle. I find comfort now in knowing that these pages are filled with lessons that I learned from her and I know that these lessons are going to change lives. Honestly, the irony is that she was not balanced, and she is one of the main reasons I feel that it is so important to strive for balance. She dealt with a lot of obstacles in her life that led her away from taking care of herself like she should have for a big portion of her life. I often wonder, would it have been any different if Tina had made it more of a priority to take care of her body, not be stressed all the time, get more sleep, have more moments of laughter and being carefree? And I often wonder whether she had any parts of her story that she wished she could have written differently. We don't know how long we have but I do know that I don't want regrets. She taught me so much, and if there is one thing I would say it is this: do what you love. Enjoy your life and strive to fill your time up with meaningful moments both in and outside the home. Time truly is fleeting.

I WILL **MANAGE MY TIME** BETTER!

1 THING I WILL CHANGE TO BECOME MORE PRODUCTIVE

☐ _____

3 DISTRACTIONS I CAN ELIMINATE

☐ _____

☐ _____

☐ _____

3 THINGS I CAN SAY NO TO

☐ _____

☐ _____

☐ _____

HOW ARE YOU SPENDING YOUR TIME?
MAP OUT A COUPLE DAYS AND SEE HOW YOU ARE USING YOUR TIME.

6 _____
7 _____
8 _____
9 _____
10 _____
11 _____
12 _____
1 _____
2 _____
3 _____
4 _____
5 _____
6 _____
7 _____
8 _____
9 _____

6 _____
7 _____
8 _____
9 _____
10 _____
11 _____
12 _____
1 _____
2 _____
3 _____
4 _____
5 _____
6 _____
7 _____
8 _____
9 _____

SEVEN

BECOME EFFICIENT

Now that you know time is your most precious commodity and you have established a schedule to help you get things done, this chapter will show you how to be even more efficient with your time. By creating workflows, and automating, outsourcing, and delegating tasks, you can focus on the things you love and on the tasks that will grant you the greatest return on investment. It is also important to have a niche or (if you own a small business) create a solution for only a narrow market. The more focused you are in your own abilities, the more value you will have.

WORKFLOWS. If you do it more than twice, create a workflow! Think about things that you do every day or every week: buying groceries and prepping meals, balancing checkbooks, editing pictures, and probably a million other tasks if you have a business. Create a workflow so that you follow the same process every single time; this will save you time and allow you to get more organized. For instance, when editing pictures I import the files in RAW to an edit folder. I cull and edit the images, and then I export them, renaming the files to YearMonthDayCustomSeq. I put that series of images into the correct folder. It is the same every single time, and I can easily search for images by date or name. This saves me time during the process, and the organization saves me time later.

If you do something on a regular basis, write down a workflow and a system that will ensure you keep it organized. Do this even for little tasks like doing laundry and dishes. Create a system that works for your life. I think everyone should write down their workflows until they become an automatic part of their day/life. How can you create workflows in the office? Where can you create workflows around your home to speed up the process of managing a household? Write it down. Once you learn the workflow it will become second nature, leaving you more organized and efficient! If you do

You can also build out content throughout the process if needed. Here are some workflow examples around the home and office:

- Keeping your home clean: sweep and wash kitchen counters (daily); mop floors, dust, clean bathrooms (weekly); strip beds (every two weeks); deep cleaning of baseboards, ceiling fans (quarterly).
- Meal prep: building menus, making grocery lists, and shopping.
- Paying bills. Pick one day a month to pay bills and reconcile your financials. Create a system for how they go into pending, paid, and then properly filed and sorted.
- At work you can create workflows for onboarding processes, how you handle requests from customers, approval processes, social media postings, and so on.

Workflows will increase productivity, assign responsibility, and create transparency if anyone else needs to step in to take over a task. Workflows ultimately help with task management; consider your time, your strengths, and your weaknesses when you build them. Here's an example of a simple workflow for taking care of personal finances on a monthly basis.

Have a list of expected bills and a preliminary budget to reference.
▼
Compile bills in a file folder.
▼
Every other Monday sort and pay bills in order of date due.
▼
Mark as paid and file bills away.
▼
Reassess preliminary budget for accuracy.
▼
Assess future monthly/quarterly budgets.

This will save you time so that you are not paying bills at the last minute or are unsure of what money is coming in or going out, and pretty soon it will become a routine.

TEMPLATES. When I think of the word "template" I think time saver! A template is something that gives you a starting point. Templates can also be a part of a workflow. I use templates a lot for marketing, design, and of course emails! I set up a workflow for answering emails and created templates to address the questions that come up a lot. Instead of retyping the same response again and again, create a template! A template is a starting point so you'll already have the basis of your message prepared, and then you can add a couple of lines to personalize the email. There are apps you can use to store notes and there are even apps that can remember template responses once you start typing them. If you are a graphic designer, templates can be created for projects or tasks that you do often. If there are groceries that you get every single week, create a template shopping list as a starting point. Create templates for anything that you do again and again.

AUTOMATION. Did someone say automation? This is when you have software or find another solution that does the job for you. For instance, I used to manually input sales receipts from our store into our accounting software. Now we have an app that does it automatically whenever a new order is received. You can automate personal bill payments. There are recurring charges that your family incurs every month, and these can be automatically paid for you. Some things that you automate will have an upfront cost or a fixed monthly cost, but you always have to take into account how much time you will be saving by automating and see if there is an ROI for the time savings.

Some other things that are useful to automate are social media posts, financial accounting, blog posting, importation of credit card transactions to accounting software, welcome emails to a new subscription, and drip campaigns. From an operations perspective, there is so much you can automate, from shipment emails to printing labels. Any time a fee is charged, if it is offset by time savings, it's worth the cost.

OUTSOURCING. I can do everything . . . nope! I've tried to do everything, and you know what? I am not good at everything. If you are trying to do everything on your own, you will just be spinning your wheels! Outsourcing means hiring an outside company to do a job or task for you, when you know that task is something you are not good at: legal stuff, accounting, design, office management, editing, and so on. There are experts in these fields who can typically take care of tasks better and more efficiently than you could if you tried to do it on your own. Your time is also really valuable, so focusing your efforts and energy on what you are good at and what gives you a competitive advantage is key. You have to put a value on your time. You might not be able to outsource tasks to begin with, but by giving yourself an hourly value, you can then start assessing whether you should outsource or not. You then ask yourself, "Is the time I would save by outsourcing this task more valuable than the money I'd save if I did it myself?" For example, I outsource cleaning my house. First, I know I am not good at it, but I also know my time will be better spent with family, organizing the garage, or doing other tasks. I also know that I started cleaning houses with my mom at age seven, and it is something that I don't particularly like.

When you outsource, you pay for services when you need them, typically for a fixed fee at the time of services, and maybe on an ongoing basis. Anything that does not give you a competitive advantage in your professional environment should be considered for outsourcing or delegating, which is my next topic. If you have the means to support it, outsource anything in the home that will free up your time to focus more on your family and building memories. This might include home maintenance, financial planning, or annual tax preparation.

DELEGATION. This is very similar to outsourcing, except you keep the job "in house." You could give a task to a family member, intern, business partner, or spouse—anyone who works in or around the household or in your professional setting. You could delegate to someone who is already doing services for you. When you delegate, you are giving responsibility for that task to someone else.

Focus on your strengths; delegate or outsource your weaknesses. I am very efficient with my time and I feel like I can work and do the tasks of two or three employees by just managing my time well, and by focusing and knowing myself. I can work a 20-hour week and be as productive as most people who work 40 hours in corporate America, all by properly managing my time as efficiently as possible and by implementing the advice above. The more you schedule and use your "efficiency skills," the more time you are going to have. The end result? Increased productivity. We get out of life what we put into it, so take a look at your daily tasks to figure out how to get more done.

FOCUS ON YOUR STRENGTHS; DELEGATE OR OUTSOURCE YOUR WEAKNESSES.

—KRISTY DICKERSON

#**START**BALANCING

LET'S BECOME **EFFICIENT!**

3 TASKS I CAN CREATE A TEMPLATE FOR

☐ _____

☐ _____

☐ _____

3 TASKS I CAN AUTOMATE

☐ _____

☐ _____

☐ _____

3 TASKS I CAN OUTSOURCE

☐ _____

☐ _____

☐ _____

3 TASKS I CAN CREATE A WORKFLOW FOR

☐ _____

☐ _____

☐ _____

TASKS I CAN DELEGATE OR OUTSOURCE RIGHT NOW

☐ _____

☐ _____

☐ _____

☐ _____

☐ _____

☐ _____

☐ _____

EIGHT

ESTABLISH HEALTHY HABITS

Health is our personal state of being. If we are healthy we have more energy to pursue passions, are happier, and can live a more full life overall. This is not only about physical health, but mental health as well. If you are not physically healthy, and mentally you don't feel good about yourself, then you will have a harder time pushing fear aside and fulfilling your destiny to reach your full potential. With physical health, consider what foods you put into your body to fuel it, how you condition it, and how you maintain it. You only have one body, and in order for you to reach your dreams you must properly take care of your most important asset: yourself. If you don't properly take care of yourself, you cannot take care of others as effectively, and you are selling yourself short.

I am going to start by saying that I am no nutritionist; I don't sell anything health-related, and I am not an expert or doctor. I am only a woman who has learned a ton about health and my own body through battling my own issues and those of my loved ones, and I have educated myself thoroughly. What I am is an advocate for living a healthy lifestyle because I know that it affects every aspect of your life. I am an advocate for understanding what is going on with your body in order to properly fuel it. For the longest time, I was filling my body with junk! I developed bad habits from a young age: I grew up with sodas in the fridge to drink at my convenience, a snack drawer that was loaded with anything I wanted, and my second helpings were considered normal in a houseful of boys. I had no knowledge of what is healthy. I don't blame my parents—this way of eating is all they knew and the snack drawer is still there in their home to this day. I just had to learn self-control and moderation. The food industry is playing a part in this as well, with toxins, hormones, and additives in our foods that research has shown trigger illnesses, diseases, and cancers. I just want our society as a whole to take health and food more seriously. From a productivity standpoint, I know that if I treat myself to real food and fuel my body properly, I can function at peak potential. Can you imagine how much more productive our society would be if everyone felt good? How much would healthy food costs be driven down if we all ate it? How much would our medical bills as a whole decrease? Health is not something you typically see discussed in a productivity book, but I feel like this is the foundation for our entire pursuit of happiness and getting things done!

HEALTH MAINTENANCE. Let's start by taking a look at physical health. We discussed scheduling self-care to make sure you are getting the medical attention and advice you need. It is vital that you make this a priority and make sure you are getting any regular screening and testing that is advised. Often when we get busy and stress comes our way, we put ourselves last. We make sure our spouse and kids don't miss appointments, but when we notice things changing in our own bodies we don't always take the time to address this. Take care of yourself—don't only solve problems when they arise, but be proactive about your own well-being. You cannot take care of others without making sure you are maintaining your body and getting the advice you need to life a long, full life. Of course, doctors can, on occasion, misdiagnose or miss something. It is imperative that you become an advocate for yourself and your body and seek answers if you know something is wrong.

FOOD AS MEDICINE. How are you fueling your body? Are you getting the nutrients you need? Have you ever heard the saying "you are what you eat"? It's true. I had to take a close look at what I was fueling my body with because it was ultimately costing me my life by harming my health and robbing me of my happiness. If we don't care for our bodies, we are exposing ourselves to disease, to a less active life, and to an unbalanced life. If you know that you are not fueling your body as you should be I advise you to seek answers, read a health book, have lunch with a friend who is good at healthy eating, or consult a nutritionist. If health is one of your goals, start by making small changes. This is hard. I know this and I really think it is not until we hit rock bottom or have something scare us that we really see the light and the importance of using food as medicine and to properly fuel our body. I want you to avoid this kind of wake-up call.

"Eating healthy is too expensive." This is something I hear often, but it is not true. Eating healthy on a budget does require you to be prepared, shop in various places, and shop in bulk, but by setting up workflows for your food you can become healthier, save money, and save time as well. Finding unprocessed foods with minimal additives is the key. Anything that comes in a box has typically been processed or modified. You have to become conscious of the foods you are eating and start paying attention to the labels on your food. If you can't pronounce an ingredient, it is typically something you should not put into your body. Our bodies were designed for raw fruits and veggies and we are all different in what we can tolerate and what we need in order to feel our best.

That all sounds great, but eating healthy and organic is expensive, right? The cost of these foods is going down every year as more companies see the growing demand. Eating healthy does take a lot more planning and prepping, but it can be done. I used to go to the grocery store to see what looked good and would build my meals at the grocery store. Without a list and a plan, I am the grocery store's target consumer. I buy anything that looks good on the endcaps, which is exactly why it is on the end: the store is marketing it to consumers. Now we plan our menus for the week and go to the grocery store with a list of ingredients that we need for our meals. I go to one or two stores once a week, knowing what I need to get where. The first couple of trips will take longer until you learn where things are and what your family likes. Since moving to organic and eating cleaner, my family has actually saved a good bit on our grocery bills because I no longer buy excess stuff that we don't need, and I am saving time running back and forth to the store. We are also all healthier, and no amount of money in the world can buy you health or more time with loved ones.

You might be saying to yourself, "this all sounds great, but I don't have time." Well, we talked about organization, time management, scheduling, and creating a workflow. You have to make time and make this a priority. It is not easy, but the benefits are life-changing. Yes, schedule it out if you need to. Your health and your family's health are worth it! I prep my green smoothies once a week and freeze them so that every night all I have to do is put one out on the kitchen counter so it's ready for me the next morning.

Physical health is closely related to mental health and I would venture to say that the majority of physical heath is a result of your diet. Try to eat real food that has not been processed. Almost everything that comes in a box has high-fructose corn syrup or sugar. There are so many companies that are pumping additives and hidden sugars into our food, even those that you might think of as healthy snacks. We are all busy, and planning ahead is the key to eating well. I knew I was not getting enough greens so I started drinking a green smoothie daily. You can use food as medicine to treat aliments and restore body functions to operate at their peak. Make your food a priority before it is too late. You are capable and worth it!

PROBIOTICS AND SUPPLEMENTS. I believe everyone should be taking probiotics, due to our environment and what we are exposed to. Probiotics are healthy bacteria that can help maintain a healthy gut. The gut is the powerhouse of our immunity and ultimately our health. At your yearly checkup, get a CBC (complete blood count) to see if you are lacking in any vitamins or supplements; this is typically also a good indicator if something else is going on. Early detection is vital for proper care. If you are lacking certain vitamins or nutrients, in my opinion, the best way to compensate for that is to find natural foods rich in that vitamin or nutrient and add it to your diet. Alternatively, you can take a high quality supplement. Our bodies require certain nutrients in order to function and if we are not getting them, our bodily functions can start derailing from their normal course.

HYDRATION. Staying properly hydrated is essential so that our bodies can do what we want. Our bodies are made up of approximately 60 percent water, and properly hydrating is important to staying productive. Dehydration has been shown to impair judgment and motor performance, and lead to a negative mood. Start your day with water. Personally, I like room temperature water and I keep a glass ready for myself every morning so that I drink as soon as I get up. Make sure that throughout the day you have water close by to keep yourself hydrated. Try adding lemons to your water—they aid digestion, boost your immune system, and can elevate your energy and mood. Studies have shown that "even mild dehydration can drain your energy and make you tired."[8] So drink up!

SUGAR. This was a hard one for me because I used to be addicted. I had to learn to break my habit of consuming too much sugar. Sugar can provide a temporary energy boost followed by a crash. There are processed sugars and natural sugars. Processed sugars, as hard as this sounds, should be eliminated from your diet. They are empty calories because they have zero nutritional value. They have been found to play a role in cancer, insulin resistance, tooth decay, and obesity; they affect your hormones and your brain. And the list goes on and on. In our society, we are not taught about the dangers that go along with sugar, but rather we are rewarded with sugar from a young age. Try to eliminate or cut down on any added sugars so that you have more energy and your body can function as it is designed to.

MEDICAL CONDITIONS OR CHRONIC PAIN. Until this is something you face you really can't grasp it completely, but there might be times in your life when you are faced with an inability to be productive or balanced. There might be a point in your life where pain or discomfort overcomes you and your only goal might be to find relief. If you are someone who has a medical condition or is faced with a temporary medical setback I want to encourage you to seek answers to get to the root of the problem, rest, and ask for help when and where you need it! We all need a tribe, or a support system, so that when life throws you a curveball, the people who are dependent on you can keep going.

My husband has the blood-clotting disorder that was discussed earlier and he also has gout, which is a type of arthritis that causes inflammation. He has to deal with both conditions and he has adapted his diet to try to live as normal a life as possible; this is now his "normal." I had a dislocated jaw once that brought on temporomandibular joint disorder and chronic myofascial pain that lasted for about two weeks. I had so much to get done, but literally the only thing I could do was try to exist from one moment to the next because the pain was so intense! I couldn't be Mom, business owner, wife, or anyone I wanted to be. I just had to buckle down, succumb to modern medicine, seek answers, and find some relief. We all face health hurdles to some degree. You might have a chronic condition that you are constantly having to monitor and deal with. You are stronger than you think you are; I want to encourage you to stay positive and work toward finding answers in order to get back to living!

EXERCISE. Of course, I can't touch on health and not talk about working out. I have gone through periods of my life when I didn't go near a gym, and other periods when I went to the gym obsessively thinking it would counteract my unhealthy habits, and I would stress when I didn't make it in one day. There are many different ways to work out, but I think it is very important to build in three to four times a week when you can burn off steam and work out your body. Working out is a way to reset your body, relieve stress, and be more productive. As reported in the *Business Insider*, "a 2011 study, published in the *Journal of Occupational and Environmental Medicine*, showed that incorporating just 2.5 hours of exercise per week into the workday led to a noticeable reduction in absences. Perhaps most importantly, fit and healthy workers are less prone to exactly the kinds of preventable, debilitating illnesses that take such a heavy toll on our families and our society."[9]

You can find a local gym, work out with friends at a local park, or even work out in the privacy of your home. The important thing is to just start moving! If I plan to go to the gym by myself or say I will work out at home it won't happen. I need someone to hold me accountable so I do group classes. I have a friend who grew up practicing gymnastics; she always trained alone and doesn't like working out in a group. Find what works best for you and stick to it! If you need someone to hold you accountable for this, find that person! Make sure you are selecting safe yet effective means to get in your exercise.

MENTAL HEALTH. My definition of mental health is how you perceive your outlook on life. If you are stressed about health, money, kids, your job, and all the other demands and pressures you are under, it can be catastrophic for your life and health. Can you eliminate stress altogether? No, but I believe by following the guidance in this book, you can take some of it away. By defining what success looks like for yourself, you can give yourself direction; by knowing who you are and what you need, you can set your schedule and allocate time; and by physically taking care of yourself, you can take care of others and get done what needs to get done. If you eat the right foods, you are going to feel better about yourself and have more energy to exert.

If you have stress in your life, find ways to control it through exercise, support, or other means. Counseling is a great way to sort through issues and talk about your problems with someone. Stress can have a negative impact on your physical health. Yoga is a great way to be physically active and mentally still your mind to become more in tune with your body. Breathing techniques can be used as well as meditation. Ultimately, by balancing your worlds, you are going to be in a more balanced mental state of mind, and happier and healthier.

SLEEP. You must have a good night's sleep in order to be productive and stay healthy. Just because I talk about waking up early doesn't mean you should sacrifice your sleep. When people feel pressed for time, sleep is typically one of the first things that goes. Not getting an adequate amount of rest has been shown to have long-term health consequences such as obesity, diabetes, and cardiovascular disease. Sleep science states that when you don't get enough sleep, your brain has a hard time staying focused; your reaction time is slower; your immune system goes downhill, leaving you exposed to sicknesses; and you feel hungrier, craving high-fat, high-calorie foods to help energize you. There are numerous other health effects, but the bottom line is that your body and your mind cannot operate at their full potential without sleep, so make it a priority.

——————————— ◇ ◇ ◇ ———————————

The most successful individuals have routines that they live by. The goal is to create routines with healthy habits that make up our days and lives. This will leave us more productive, more balanced, healthier, and happier. Routines create structure and give us guidelines and parameters to operate within, which can eliminate stress and set expectations. They relieve us from having to think about our schedules or our habits, and rather allow us to just work, giving us more focus. We create routines that dictate how we spend our time and live out our lives. When consistency is established through a routine that is healthy and productive, success can follow. Habits and routines ultimately become a system for your life. They give you a rhythm . . . you just have to find the right beat.

We all have good and bad habits that we carry with us, and some of those habits take root from a young age. This chapter deals with a lot of the topics that we have already discussed; if you establish healthy routines, you will not only be able to balance your pursuits better, but build a life full of more energy and intentional moments. To review, here are some healthy habits that you must adopt to be the most productive version of yourself:

- Establish an exercise routine.
- Eat healthy meals and snacks throughout the day.
- Start your day with water and make sure you stay hydrated throughout the day.
- Say no to anything that doesn't align with your personal or professional goals so that you are not overcommitted, causing stress.
- Organize and clean your office space, as well as all the other spaces where you live so that clutter doesn't stress you out. When cleaning, eliminate any health triggers or unhealthy options that would tempt you to cheat.

- Schedule in medical appointments to make sure you are taking care of any needs your body may have.
- Schedule in times to destress, which might include taking breaks.
- Get a good night's rest.
- Maintain social interactions so that you are balanced, controlling stress and contributing to your mental health.
- Plan for success. Set time aside to plan for your health.
- Have people who you can lean on for support, for knowledge, and for accountability.
- Stop thinking so much and start doing! Small accomplishments add up!

By creating healthy habits, you will transform your body and your mind, and in turn you will transform your entire outlook on life, increasing your confidence and your drive. Think about all the other chapters in this book; health habits are what fuels you to do everything we have been talking about. You and your loved ones deserve to get the best, most energetic version of you—mind and body. Like everything else in *Start Balancing*, this is all about creating healthy habits, moderation, and balance. Taking care of your health is vital to being your best self. I know firsthand that this is one of the hardest things to do. On the next page, you will find an assessment worksheet to determine where you are currently, both physically and mentally, along with actions steps to get to where you want to be.

ESTABLISH **HEALTHY HABITS**

MY BIGGEST HEALTH CHALLENGE IS. . .

_____

_____

_____

3 THINGS I CAN CUT TO BE MORE HEALTHY

☐ _____

☐ _____

☐ _____

3 THINGS I CAN ADD TO BE MORE HEALTHY

☐ _____

☐ _____

☐ _____

HEALTHY HABITS I WILL ESTABLISH AS A ROUTINE

MENTAL HEALTH

☐ _____ DUE DATE ___ / ___ / ___

☐ _____ DUE DATE ___ / ___ / ___

☐ _____ DUE DATE ___ / ___ / ___

☐ _____ DUE DATE ___ / ___ / ___

☐ _____ DUE DATE ___ / ___ / ___

PHYSICAL HEALTH

☐ _____ DUE DATE ___ / ___ / ___

☐ _____ DUE DATE ___ / ___ / ___

☐ _____ DUE DATE ___ / ___ / ___

☐ _____ DUE DATE ___ / ___ / ___

☐ _____ DUE DATE ___ / ___ / ___

NINE

BUILD COMMUNITY AND RELATIONSHIPS

SURROUND YOURSELF

WITH THE DREAMERS AND THE DOERS,

THE BELIEVERS AND THE THINKERS,

BUT MOST OF ALL,

SURROUND YOURSELF

WITH THOSE WHO SEE GREATNESS

WITHIN YOU

EVEN WHEN YOU DON'T SEE IT YOURSELF.

—EDMUND LEE

#STARTBALANCING

We all learn, grow, and flourish by having individuals in our lives who help support, guide, and lead us. We are also happier when we have a tribe of people who are part of our lives and part of our success. I could have titled this chapter "Networks" or "Support," but I think "Community" is a much better term. Even if you are introverted, you will have a greater chance of success and be happier having others to share your life with and cheer you on. There will be times when you need that support and that backbone of community to push you forward as you embark on your mission, and there will also be times when you need that tribe of individuals to help you carry some weight.

Think of yourself as a tree. If you are alone standing in the wind you could get blown over, but if you have strong roots helping you to weather the storm, those roots (family, friends, and community) hold you stronger than you could hold yourself. Your roots are what keep you deeply grounded. No matter how strong you think you are you will have moments where you will need your "roots." Can a community also be someone that holds you accountable? Yes, of course, but community is there for so much more. If you become a parent, your world will drastically change and you are going to need a support system. That system will include the people you immediately surround yourself with and who know you best: spouse, kids, family, parents, and friends will provide the support and encouragement that is so important to weather any storms that arise.

If you are around people who are negative and never upbeat about their own lives, that can be toxic for your life. I cannot stress how important it is to eliminate toxic people from your day-to-day interactions. Surround yourself with people who encourage and inspire you! You need a community of friends or colleagues who are constantly pushing you to be the best version of yourself. A positive community can advance your career, help you through a rough time, and ultimately change your life. I know for a fact that without my tribe I would not be writing this book and I would not be the woman that I am. Without having those people as I build a lifetime of memories, I would not be as happy as I am.

Where and how do you find community? You have to insert yourself into community. You have to show up and make conversation, regardless of how shy you might be. Join classes at the gym, join a team, join societies or sororities, volunteer for different organizations, attend networking events, get involved in a group with a shared hobby—the list could go on and on. You will expand your community by being social.

Work out in group exercise classes; typically you will find like-minded individuals at the gym. The people I work out with at the local gym all have different schedules that go a million different ways, but for an hour we connect with each other and burn some calories. There is a group of guys at my gym that meets three days a week to play basketball, and there are tennis teams all around. Join a church, attend a spiritual organization, or get involved in a small group. Attend neighborhood or community functions. Go with someone else that you already know so it will be easier to talk to others.

Something that you should never stop doing is meeting others and networking. Whether you work in a corporate setting, own your own business, or are a stay-at-home parent, networking and meeting others can open up so many opportunities. I am not just talking about going to networking events, but getting involved and going to dinners at conferences. Yes, of course, any seminars, workshops, or networking opportunities are great too. The more intimate the setting, the better the opportunity you have to get to know others on a more personal level, and what I really enjoy is getting past the small talk. If I look back on the businesses I have started, my networks are what allowed me to generate enough profit to take my businesses to the next level. If I look back on the hardest times in my life, community is what has inspired me to keep going and helped me when I couldn't do it on my own.

I generally enjoy meeting people. I love hearing other people's stories and how they have navigated their life. It is important to not just meet people but to get to know them. I would say I am a homebody and I refer to myself as an extroverted introvert. You put me in a room full of people I don't know, and you will find me migrating to the food table, but once I am comfortable I am good to go. I am a people person and for me it is uplifting and inspiring to be around others who are like-minded and to be a part of their journey. It is important to surround yourself with others that inspire and challenge you!

There are also easy ways to network and associate through community from the comfort of your home, via online forums, Facebook groups, or social media platforms. This is also an important way to quickly and easily stay connected to others who have similar interests. These platforms are great for quick answers and when you need to reach out for help. Do not discount the value of in-person meetings and relationship building, but online interactions are a great way to feel and stay connected. Don't isolate yourself; find community wherever you can. You will need your tribe to help you continue pushing yourself to be your best self.

BUILDING **RELATIONSHIPS**

3 AREAS WHERE I HAVE A STRONG SUPPORT SYSTEM

☐ _____

☐ _____

☐ _____

HOW CAN I FURTHER INVEST IN THESE?

☐ _____

☐ _____

☐ _____

☐ _____

☐ _____

☐ _____

3 AREAS WHERE I AM LACKING COMMUNITY

☐ _____

☐ _____

☐ _____

HOW CAN I IMPROVE THESE RELATIONSHIPS?

☐ _____

☐ _____

☐ _____

☐ _____

☐ _____

☐ _____

TEN

TAKE BREAKS

Living intentionally is something that is hard to do. With all the demands on us, it is hard to take time away from your normal routine, but taking breaks and scheduling downtime is imperative in order to *Start Balancing*. Taking a break can be as simple as walking away from the computer and meeting your mom or friends for lunch. It could also be more involved, like a vacation. Taking breaks can reduce stress and give you a renewed sense of energy to complete the tasks at hand. Recent studies show that those who give in to some kind of diversion and take breaks tend to perform better than those who don't.[1]

Taking breaks helps you to avoid burnout. If you are working under a lot of stress, it can wreak havoc on your entire body and mind. Taking both mental and physical breaks can give you a renewed sense of focus and remind you why you do what you do. We often wear multiple hats, put in long hours, and eventually will start running on steam, resulting in burnout. When you are depleted, productivity will decline and you will be slower to solve tasks. Here are some ways to incorporate breaks into your schedule:

DAILY BREAKS. Take short work breaks throughout your day to break up your normal routine. One study found that mental fatigue takes hold after three hours of continuous time on task, while other studies suggest it happens after 90 minutes. When scheduling these breaks, you should take into account how you normally feel throughout the day and how long you can typically perform at a top notch. Do you typically have an afternoon slump? Mid-morning, do you hit a wall? Getting to know yourself and how you feel throughout the day is important so you can intentionally schedule in breaks in order to stay feeling your best and performing at your peak. Small breaks throughout the day could be going on a coffee run, taking a break to meet someone for lunch, or stepping outside with some water to get some fresh air. You could also take a break to get some physical exercise in. Studies have shown that a moderate level of cardio activity can boost creativity and productivity for two hours afterward, so consider using your lunch break to get moving.[11]

UNPLUGGED WEEKENDS. Schedule unplugged weekends in order to mentally and physically reset. Go hiking, rent a house and share it with friends, visit local attractions, try some DIY tasks around the house, go to a festival or event, or anything that you will look forward to, and disconnect from your work devices for the weekend. Electronic devices are a blessing and curse. Fifty years ago, when employees left work they left completely, but now with smartphones and computers we can take our work with us virtually anywhere we go. We can have it with us on the weekend, in our exercise class, on vacation, and even during family dinner. You must practice self-control and learn not to constantly check your devices and be on call all the time.

VACATIONS. Schedule trips or breaks in your routine that you look forward to; when you come back you will feel refreshed! Time off does your mind, body, and soul good. Personally I like to really seek adventure, which forces me to completely disconnect! This is also a way to give undivided attention to the loved ones you are traveling with. A recent survey of worker productivity and vacation by the *Harvard Business Review* found that in nations with more paid vacation, people had a slightly higher tendancy to work faster, stay focused longer, and even feel more impatient.[12] Yes, vacations can be fun but it also seems that fully disconnecting and taking those breaks can leave you more productive in the office by forcing you to be more organized and on top of things. Vacations can give you time to recharge and, in my opinion, the best vacations leave you ready to get back to your life!

TAKING TIME TO LIVE AND RECHARGE WILL ONLY INSPIRE YOU TO WORK.

—KRISTY DICKERSON

#**START**BALANCING

WORKWEEK. Jobs with flexible work hours have been shown to increase productivity because workers are happier overall. Employees now more than ever are attracted to jobs that give them a sense of responsibility; being able to control their own schedule gives them a sense of ownership. Our employees work a four-day workweek, giving them a three-day weekend every weekend. Four-day workweeks are shown to increase productivity and force everyone to take a break. For a mom, that means an extra day to plan, schedule, and get in appointments that are needed, without having to miss work. For me, it is also a day to take the occasional day date with my husband, spend time with kids, or wrap up loose ends in the office without distractions. A shortened week doesn't work for everyone, but are there ways that you can get more flexibility to balance personal and professional endeavors throughout the week?

TOO MANY BREAKS. I also want to address this. Haven't we all fallen victim to a Netflix series? You know, where every spare moment is given to finding out what will happen next? Try to limit your television time and time doing other things that are not productive. Taking breaks is a good thing but when they become all-consuming, they take away from your productivity both inside and outside the home. Moderation is the key here, as it is in everything. If you know you struggle with this, set a timer for your breaks. When the timer goes off, it is time to go back to being productive.

Often when you set aside time for yourself, it is accompanied by guilt, especially if you are a parent. It is important that you have a no-guilt attitude, and give yourself some grace.

Taking breaks will leave you feeling refreshed and more energetic. If you are balanced there is no reason for guilt. By taking care of yourself and having a no-guilt mind-set, you will be able to approach life and tasks with a greater wholeness. Whether those breaks are short bursts throughout the day, weekend getaways, or longer vacations, our bodies need downtime and they need time to rest in order to increase mental focus. Get recharged, work smarter, and fully engage with your loved ones and your life.

ACTIONS/PLACES THAT RECHARGE ME

- [ ]
- [ ]
- [ ]
- [ ]
- [ ]
- [ ]
- [ ]
- [ ]

3 THINGS I WILL DO FOR ME THIS WEEK

☐ _____

☐ _____

☐ _____

3 THINGS I WILL DO FOR ME THIS MONTH

☐ _____

☐ _____

☐ _____

3 THINGS I WILL DO FOR ME THIS YEAR

☐ _____

☐ _____

☐ _____

ELEVEN

OVERCOME OBSTACLES

Everything that we have talked about up to this point, when implemented, will help you to be more productive, continuing to move your life forward. You have taken a good look in the mirror and found out who you are and what you need to be happy. You have clearly defined success and outlined your goals to get you there. You have gotten organized, you are focused, you are practicing your time management skills, and you are now more efficient. You have created healthy habits that are life-changing and are surrounding yourself with healthy relationships that hold you accountable. You are taking breaks when you need to and ultimately you are balancing your worlds. By planning and doing everything outlined in this book you will be the best version of yourself.

What happens when you can't? What happens when you are faced with an obstacle that derails your focus and doesn't allow you to be healthy, and balance becomes a fleeting thought? What happens when you lose that dream job you worked so hard for? What happens when life as you'd planned it doesn't really pan out like you hoped? I hope for your sake this chapter doesn't become the most important chapter, but I want you to be prepared because obstacles will present themselves in all forms. I have been faced with numerous obstacles that forced me to change, to grow, and to seek help at times. Planning, having a support system, and doing everything outlined in this book will help you to continue to press on when an obstacle arises. Obstacles can be internal or external. Internal obstacles are things that you do to yourself that affect your ability to balance and be happy. External obstacles are things that happen to you beyond your control.

The biggest internal obstacles are our own bad habits and bad choices. One of the biggest obstacles we have to face is learning to control fear and believing in ourselves. We often become complacent and the only thing that is standing between us and our goals is, well, us. By creating a plan, having people hold you accountable, and being organized you are equipped to lessen your fear, but this doesn't make it go away. You have to believe, and when disappointment happens, let it go. You will make mistakes. Failing at things and making mistakes is where you learn. These are all obstacles that we create for ourselves and a lot of times they have consequences. If you are not making healthy eating choices and taking care of your personal well-being, over time you will start to see this manifest as physical problems. If you make a bad judgment call at work and cost the company time or money, there could be repercussions. In my opinion, internal obstacles are the best types of obstacles to face because you can change them and learn from them. One of the best ways to do this is through seeking knowledge, and part of that knowledge will be gained by making mistakes—this is where growth will happen!

Sometimes things that you cannot control might happen in your life. You might feel as if you are a victim of circumstance or you might feel as if life does not seem fair. External obstacles force change on you, and you must overcome them even though you feel as if you did nothing to deserve them. This could be related to health, genetics, or bad circumstances; the economy could cause major obstacles in your career path or financial success. I am going to go through some of the major internal and external obstacles that can affect you so that you can be prepared. Recovering from these types of obstacles may require time, professional intervention, or (in most cases) your community and relationships, that tribe of people who will be vital for weathering the storms around you.

CAREER CHANGE. Have you ever lost your job? If you have, you know there is no such thing as job security. This could be an internal or external obstacle, depending on the circumstance. I believe that you should always have an up-to-date resume in its best possible condition, and also a current headshot. You should constantly be educating yourself and learning so that your skill set continues to grow in order to stay on top of trends and stay relevant. Your relationships and your network will be most valuable to you when trying to advance your career or if you lose your job.

When experiencing job loss, the most important thing you can do is to be social and continue to build in-person relationships. Do you know anyone who works at the firm where you want to apply, and could you meet them for lunch? Have you stopped by to meet HR with your resume in hand? Do your business networking sites have up-to-date images and information? Are you continuing your education and getting the extra training needed to advance your career? Doing these things will give you a starting point in the event that job loss does occur, allowing you to speed up the employment process. If you are actively searching for a job, what are some steps that you can take to make yourself more desirable and increase your chances? I believe the answer is going the extra mile by being diligent and making sure you are following up, dropping by in-person, and being thorough with your resume.

HEALTH ISSUES. Sometimes we are just not physically or mentally capable of functioning or operating at our normal capacity. We all face different medical issues that can be short- or long-term and may prevent us from doing the things we want to. You might have had a health issue from birth, and your normal is inherently different from everyone else's. It is imperative to focus on creating healthy habits as discussed in Chapter 8, so that you don't bring a health problem on yourself and create an internal obstacle due to bad choices. Health issues can cause stress and anxiety and my best advice here is to rest when your body needs it, lean on your relationships, seek counsel if needed, and make sure you have someone to hold you accountable if you know unhealthy habits are one of your weaknesses. Don't be afraid to ask for help. You must be proactive in seeking any answers you may need in order to get to the root of issues, so organization and routine checkups are crucial.

Health issues can also affect your loved ones, which can derail your plans and create an obstacle. My aunt suddenly became really sick in her thirties. She had two young kids and my family rallied for her. She never spent the night alone in the hospital in the eight months she was sick. Her two young girls were cared for, and we all rotated staying with my aunt. My other aunt, Deanna, was a bone marrow match and I was a platelet match, and we both donated in the hope that it would save her and bring her back home. As you read earlier, she didn't win her fight against cancer. We only have one family and family is not always just blood. When health issues arise, either for yourself or for loved ones, they will affect your focus and productivity. I want that to be an expectation. It is important that you ask for help or be the help, prioritize, reset, and reassess goals if needed. "The hustle" will still be there and it is okay to take a break and focus your energy and efforts on yourself or loved ones.

FEAR. Do you know how many times I almost gave up on my dream of writing this book? Will anyone read it? What will others think? I am pouring my heart and every ounce of myself into this book, exposing myself to everything I am afraid of. I am not perfect. At times I am a mediocre mom, wife, and friend, and I want you to know this about me. I am a small-town girl from the suburbs who spends most of my days in yoga pants striving to balance motherhood and chasing my dreams. I want to remind you that you are enough, in your pursuit of your dreams and in what you are currently doing. I chose to

DON'T LET YOUR
FEARS STOP

YOU

FROM BEING WHO

YOU

ARE MEANT TO BE.

—KRISTY DICKERSON

#STARTBALANCING

write and to share because although you and I might have very different personalities and come from very different backgrounds, all of these principles apply equally to each of us. Your fears and my fears are the same. Acceptance, happiness, contentment, and success are all things that I think we not only deserve but should strive for. You have to be confident in yourself and in your ability. I know I am meant to write this book, to share, and to teach, and I really believe that my life circumstances and knowledge have brought me to this purpose. My "why" is to impact as many lives as possible and I am not letting fear stop me. Don't let this confidence overshadow the fact that daily I am fearful. Over time I have just learned to embrace it, and control my fear by having a support system and continuing to educate myself so I am not blindly making poor decisions. Don't let fear stop you from doing the things you were meant to do. Remember your why, and turn to your community to support you and cheer for you when doubt tries to seep in.

MOTIVATION. You know you want to make a change but you just keep procrastinating. Why? Why wait until Monday, or next month, or why wait until the new year? I will tell you why: your brain is working against you. Our human nature is to confine ourselves to our comfortable routines and the reality is that it is hard for us to act and to bring change to our lives. You are motivated, you know you want it, but taking those first steps is just so hard. *Will it change my life drastically? Will I fail? Is it the right time?* We ask ourselves all these questions. You might feel overwhelmed; you don't know where to start so instead of acting, paralysis takes over. Sometimes you procrastinate because you can't decide. Just make a decision. As I always say, stop thinking, and start doing!

Break goals down into mini-goals to make them less intimidating. Sharing your goals with someone else is an important part of motivation. Who did you ask to hold you accountable for this goal? We are more likely to let ourselves down than to let down others—this is why you need to share! Motivation is something that really cannot be taught. You just have to have the grit and the desire to make it happen. Start rolling up your sleeves.

GRIEF/SHOCK/CHANGE. Grief, shock, and change can all be really hard to deal with. We find comfort in routine and in the relationships that surround us, but what happens if life throws you an obstacle that changes it all? This obstacle could be a death, a divorce, a loss of identity, or really any unplanned event that rocks your world or forces you to change. It can be debilitating, and can lead to depression. I know this firsthand. I have unexpectedly lost loved ones when cancer has struck, I have been forced to give up my dreams to fight for my husband's life, and I have failed at tasks throughout my life. I am still learning the art of balancing motherhood and entrepreneurship. I am forced to change and grow daily.

Grief can result from anything that brings a feeling of loss and during these times I would like to remind you of one thing: I don't think time heals all wounds, but it does make them better. You can find a new routine and purpose, but you have to seek this out. The community that we discussed earlier is what will help you overcome these obstacles in your life. During these times, give yourself some grace and intentionally fill your schedule with tasks and things to do to take your mind off your circumstances. For an entire year of my life I was depressed, and people were telling me that I was, but I honestly didn't think it was true. Looking back, I was isolating myself and just going through the motions of life. I was depressed and it took time and perspective to see this. Lean on others for support, be intentional with your time, and take care of yourself. We often don't understand the "why" of life's events but I fully believe that there is a purpose and a reason for everything that happens to us, both the good and the bad.

FAMILY OBLIGATIONS. Family is everything and we would do anything for them. Sometimes family brings on obligations and commitments that we would not otherwise have. It requires our time and effort and doesn't always allow us to balance our worlds or chase our dreams. I describe family as an obstacle to balancing because this can be a very true statement for you at some point in your life, or indefinitely.

Consider whether this is a season. Do you have young kids who will grow up or do you have a sick family member who you are helping to get better? If this is just a season, remember that. Or is it something more long-term? Have your parents gotten older and will they need your care from now on? Maybe your child was born with special needs or had an accident and needs long-term care. Is the family obstacle rooted in financial needs, time commitments, or emotional stress? Likely it will be all three. This is what family and your tribe is for; we would do anything for them, but you need a plan for yourself and the circumstances. Don't let guilt hold you back from making a decision. The answer to these questions might also be sacrifice. Your selfless act might be to take on the responsibility for a family member because you know this is your calling or the only answer. This is not easy and it is okay to sometimes feel anger and guilt associated with it. Knowing these obligations, you can create SMART goals to set yourself up to succeed no matter the circumstances. If you are dealing with a long-term obligation, it is important that you create goals, have plans in place, assign responsibility to other parties, create a financial plan, and remember that even when taking care of family it is paramount that you take care of yourself, both mentally and physically. You must not sacrifice your health.

FINANCIAL SETBACKS. We have discussed the organization of money and the importance of accountability, saving, and planning, but for so many people, financial obstacles are still present. Financial setbacks can be debilitating and all-consuming, and can affect your health and other areas of your life. Brett Wilder, author of *The Quiet Millionaire*, states that there are seven obstacles to financial success, and we are going to review these seven obstacles and how they relate to productivity and bringing balance to your world.[13]

1. **Lack of discipline.** We talked about this earlier and why you need to be sure you create a plan. I think discipline is typically not there if you have no benchmarks to hold yourself up to. You also have no reason for self-control if you are not working toward a bigger goal. Make sure you have someone in your life to celebrate these victories with.

2. **Materialism.** Buying things will not buy happiness. In the short term, this might give you a little satisfaction, but by clearly defining success and living a more minimalist life you can shift your thinking. Don't compare your success or your "haves" to anyone else's.

3. **Debt.** This needs to be avoided at all costs and it takes discipline. Remember that financial leverage can be beneficial, but debt is never a good thing and it just leads to stress and obligations to pay others.

4. **Taxes.** Have a knowledgeable advisor help you build your budget and understand your taxes. If you don't know what to expect or how you could be lessening your tax

burden, you will never plan for this. Taxes are not something that you should only think about once a year; there should be an ongoing process to understand, save, and know what you need to pay so that you don't incur debt to Uncle Sam.

5. **Inflation.** Inflation is when things continue to cost more, meaning we pay more in our daily lives. Actively planning your financials on an ongoing basis will help you to understand which aspects of your budget may require more of your money.

6. **Investment mistakes.** You might make mistakes, spend money or time on an investment that ultimately doesn't pay off. You learn from failures, seek knowledge, and when a mistake is made, you make a plan to avoid it in the future and to recoup as much of the loss as possible. You also have to learn, in some instances, to let it go. If you made a mistake and created your own financial obstacle, you can't be so hard on yourself that you cause yourself stress. There were likely external obstacles that you couldn't control, such as the economy, that affected your financial investment. Diversifying your assets is one of the best ways to ensure that, overall, you will have a sound portfolio.

7. **Emergencies.** Every obstacle covered in this chapter can result in a financial burden. Your inability to work, a death, a divorce, an unplanned pregnancy, a job loss, or an HVAC system failing in your home are all things that you don't necessarily plan for but can happen. It is important that you have insurance, create an emergency account so that when life does throw you an obstacle, from a financial perspective, you are able to tackle it head on.

If money and financial planning are weak points for you, that is okay. It is important to acknowledge this—know this is a weakness of yours, and seek help and accountability to establish a plan so it's no longer an obstacle. So many goals require money to make them happen and it is paramount that this is an area of your life that you plan for so that it is not a constant obstacle.

We will all face obstacles to varying degrees during our life. Don't get discouraged. It is okay to take it one day at a time instead of worrying about the week, month, or year ahead. There will be obstacles in our lives at various times and this will serve as a reminder of how lucky we truly are and that we must start balancing to savor the good days and the "good stuff." Focus on the wins, not the losses, even if a win is as simple as getting out of the bed and taking a shower, going for a ten-minute walk, or sending a resume. Small steps add up to big accomplishments and you might just need time to heal.

We must build a life full of intentional moments because it really is the only way to live, and sometimes one of the best things we can do when facing obstacles is to give and channel our energy toward someone else. Find ways to encourage someone else; sometimes knowing that others are facing the same challenges establishes common ground and a level of comfort. Your hardships can be used to help someone else who is going through a similar experience. So each day look for an opportunity to bless someone else's life. Whether your obstacle is internal or external, having a plan to overcome it is what you will need. You also have to learn when to give yourself some grace and when to push yourself out of your comfort zone even if you don't feel ready. We only have one body, one mind, and one life to live. This life is short, so be grateful for your path wherever it may be leading you.

CURRENTLY, MY BIGGEST OBSTACLE IS. . .

HOW DO I PLAN TO OVERCOME IT?

HUSTLE

TO MOVE THE WORLD, WE MUST FIRST MOVE OURSELVES.

—SOCRATES (5TH CENTURY BC)

#STARTBALANCING

The last chapter, and I know you are ready. Nothing in life is ever going to be given to you: it is up to you to make your dreams come true. I want these chapters to serve as a road map for how to *Start Balancing* your worlds and allow yourself to be as productive as possible. This will ultimately leave you space to build a life full of intentional and meaningful moments both inside and outside of the office and the home. You are responsible for your own destiny and no one is going to push you or give you permission to chase your dreams fearlessly.

I don't want you to finish this book thinking that balance is always achieved, because it is not. I am not always balanced, but here I am sharing my life and heart with you because I believe that the pursuit of balance is where you will find happiness. It is something that I continually strive for on a daily basis, as I want you to as well. I feel guilty at times, I get sick, I make mistakes, and I have to lean on people for support. For me, not understanding and not pursuing balance has almost cost me my marriage and my identity, and it was certainly costing me my time. Our time is really all we have. We have one life to live and one chance at making an impact and getting it right. How we chose to spend our time will become our legacy. There will be some days when you feel like you own it and other days when you will wish you could start over—this is normal and part of the growth process that will never really end.

Balance will have seasons that coincide with the hustle. I look at the last ten years of my life and I realize there have been seasons for hustle on my personal ambitions, seasons for hustle on my professional ambitions, and seasons when I have been able to balance them all. When you are out of balance, ultimately something suffers and often it is your happiness and yourself. I want to remind you that seasons are just that. They are temporary, and another season is upon the horizon—you might just have to embrace it and do the work necessary to get you through.

Try to avoid feeling overwhelmed. Even if you have a passion for something, you will burn out if you don't find balance. There needs to be an end in sight or a clear vision of where you are going and why. You will only be able to operate without balance for so long before your performance starts declining in the office or your home life starts to suffer. If you are running on a hamster wheel and it is not just for a season, it might be time for you to make a change in your life.

I also want to remind you that there is never a perfect time for change. We don't get green lights in our lives giving us permission to go. Is there ever a perfect time to start a family, ask for a promotion, or take a workshop on that hobby you have been wanting to take up? You just have to start! You must chase your dreams! You have to be your own advocate. We ultimately don't know how much time we are afforded and there is no such thing as perfect timing, or perfect anything for that matter. I believe there are moments of intentional living that add up to a life well lived.

It is important that when doing your hustle, you remind yourself of your "why" and celebrate the small victories on a daily basis. We have to hustle to make our dreams a reality. Is the thing you are lacking grit? Are you scared? Do you want to do something more with your life but don't know where to start? These words and worksheets are just that unless they are accompanied by action. I want to see you rolling up your sleeves and doing what you are capable of. Your dreams are worth fighting for. *You* are worth fighting for and you were uniquely designed to do something big. Sometimes you just have to stop thinking and start doing! The knowledge taught in this book will amount to nothing if you don't apply it!

What I do know is that good old-fashioned work is the only thing that will get you where you want to be: hopping out of bed bright and early, getting callused hands, making mistakes, admitting mistakes, apologizing to your loved ones, asking for help, and picking yourself back up and going again. Perseverance is something that I cannot teach you—and really no one can. It is something that comes from deep within. People tell me all the time that I am lucky in life. You know, the harder I work the more "luck" I seem to come across. I don't believe in luck; I believe in opportunities that you are prepared for. I feel as though I have had a lot of odds stacked against me, and I know you have felt the same.

A lot of people say you can't pursue your professional passion, have children, be healthy, and have time for your family and friends. They say you can pick three and one will suffer. There are articles and major publications stating this. I completely disagree. You have to have priorities, be productive with your time, system, and people in place to support you, and be willing to work for it. Be efficient, make healthy living part of your routine, and if you are diligent with your schedule and set hard boundaries between your home life and work life, balance can be achieved. Ultimately, to be balanced you have to be driven, learn self-control, and be intentional with your time.

The path that I am suggesting you might be destined for has no road map. It is not easy. We are not given a manual that tells us how we should operate and with whom. Life is filled with uncertainty and you truly only get out of it what you put into it. If you have not already completed the chapter worksheets, I want you to do so now.

Hustle is what we have to do in order to make our dreams come true. It is what we have to do in order to build a life full of intentional and meaningful moments. I feel it is what

DATE
WORKSHEETS
COMPLETED

☐   /   /   Know Yourself

☐   /   /   Define Success

☐   /   /   Be Accountable

☐   /   /   Get Organized

☐   /   /   Get Focused

☐   /   /   Manage Your Time

☐   /   /   Become Efficient

☐   /   /   Establish Healthy Habits

☐   /   /   Build Community and Relationships

☐   /   /   Take Breaks

☐   /   /   Overcome Obstacles

Hustle!

we are obligated to do, not only for ourselves, but for everyone around us. Happiness is achieved when your definition of success is met. I want to thank you for sharing your life with me and for reading. I want to remind you that you are unique and that you were designed to have a place and a purpose and you have to seek it out. I also want to encourage you and say that you can do anything you put your mind to. I want you to *Start Balancing*—not tomorrow, not next Monday, or next year, but right now!

YOU'VE GOT THIS!

FOR ADDITIONAL INFORMATION & FREE PDF DOWNLOADS
www.**Start**Balancing.com/downloads

NOTES

1. "New Years Resolution Statistics." Statistic Brain, http://www.statisticbrain.com/new-years-resolution-statistics/

2. Joseph Carroll, "Time Pressures, Stress Common for Americans." http://www.gallup.com/poll/103456/time-pressures-stress-common-americans.aspx

3. Christine DiGangi, "A Whopping 80 Percent of Americans Are in Debt." MSN, http://www.msn.com/en-us/news/money/a-whopping-80-percent-of-americans-are-in-debt/ar-BBllyhK

4. "A Look at the Shocking Student Loan Debt Statistics for 2017." Student Loan Hero, https://studentloanhero.com/student-loan-debt-statistics/

5. Sean Williams, "Baby Boomers' Retirement Woes Summed Up in 5 Statistics." The Motley Fool, https://www.fool.com/retirement/general/2016/05/15/baby-boomers-retirement-woes-summed-up-in-5-statis.aspx

6. Brother, "'P-Touch® Means Business' Survey Reveals Offices Waste More Than $177 Billion Per Year Looking for Lost Items." http://www.brother-usa.com/PressReleases/P-Touch%20Means%20Business%20Press%20Release.pdf

7. Kristin Wong, "How Long it Takes to Get Back on Track After a Distraction." http://lifehacker.com/how-long-it-takes-to-get-back-on-track-after-a-distract-1720708353

8. Mayo Clinic, "Water: How Much Should You Drink Every Day?" http://www.mayoclinic.org/healthy-lifestyle/nutrition-and-healthy-eating/in-depth/water/art-20044256

9. Ryan Holmes, "Why It's Time We Paid Employees to Exercise at Work." Business Insider, http://www.businessinsider.com/why-its-time-we-paid-employees-to-exercise-at-work-2015-3

10. "Brief Diversions Vastly Improve Focus, Researchers Find." ScienceDaily, https://www.sciencedaily.com/releases/2011/02/110208131529.htm

11. David M. Blanchette, Stephen P. Ramocki, John N. O'del and Michael S. Casey, "Aerobic Exercise and Creative Potential: Immediate and Residual Effects." http://www.ric.edu/faculty/dblanchette/exercisearticle.htm

12. Jack Zenger and Joseph Folkman, "Are We More Productive When We Have More Time Off?" *Harvard Business Review*, https://hbr.org/2015/06/are-we-more-productive-when-we-have-more-time-off?

13. J.D. Roth, "7 Obstacles to Financial Success." *Time*, http://business.time.com/2011/08/26/7-obstacles-to-financial-success/

YOU ARE CAPABLE OF AMAZING THINGS.

—KRISTY DICKERSON

#STARTBALANCING

If you are reading this, you have made it to the end. This book is short and precise and it's designed to be clean, small, and evenly shaped—all precisely driving home my message. You are capable of so much and you don't even realize it. This book can either light a fire under you to put dreams into action, or it can now sit on a shelf as part of your decor because it is so pretty. I want action, I want change, I want you to be pushed out of your comfort zone. I think pure happiness is found in pursuing your dreams, having a strong support system to help get you there, and knowing who you are and what you need to be happy. You can balance your worlds. I shared a huge piece of my heart and my passion in this book and I hope you are inspired to get busy!

Thank you for reading.

Kristy Dickerson

ABOUT THE AUTHOR

Kristy Dickerson, mom of three boys, keynote speaker, businesswoman, active CEO, and co-founder of STARTplanner, has devoted her life to providing hope for individuals looking to achieve balance, success, and happiness in their lives. Dickerson is a sought-after keynote speaker thanks to her relatable story, valuable advice, no-excuses attitude, and upbeat personality, which she instills in all aspects of her brands. She believes and preaches that individuals have the ability to do anything they want. Featured in *Forbes*, *Entrepreneur*, and Inc.com among others, Dickerson is a powerhouse, showing others how to be productive and make things happen.

ACKNOWLEDGMENTS

Jesus. For saving me, being my pillar of strength, and for your ultimate sacrifice.

Jeremy. For loving me, sticking with me through thick and thin, and pushing me to be the best version of myself. I love our life we have built. I'm proud of you, and all that I am today is because of your support. Love you.

My boys, Roman, August, and Silas. For making me a mom, grounding me, and giving me a reason to constantly strive to be more for you. I love you to the moon and back, and you are my greatest accomplishment.

Mom. For always nurturing and pouring into me, and for showing me what it means to be a strong independent woman. Love you.

Dad. For your work ethic and strength. For always showing me that nothing in life comes to you without working for it. Love you.

Grandma and Grandpa. For always cheering for me and thinking I was awesome, even when I wasn't. Grandma, you are missed dearly. Love you both.

Nana and Papa. For showing me how simplicity is beautiful. Your devotion to each other and your family is enduring. Love you both.

Jenny. For being my creative counterpart, my accountability, and for believing in me and fearlessly chasing dreams alongside me from across the country! We did it.

START team. For your hard work and big dreams. We are impacting lives throughout the country because of your talent. You are the reason I've been able to find balance in my life and encourage others to do the same.

My village. My community. My people. If you're reading this and you know me, thank you. You are a part of me—it is these people, these lives that I get to be a part of that are my inspiration. Without your support, your guiding hand in my life, and your influence, I would not the person I am today.

Are you ready to dig deeper?

It's time to put pen to paper. . .

Organization is the cornerstone to setting yourself up to succeed. STARTplanner helps you to define your goals in all areas of your life and guides you with actionable steps that carry over to monthly and daily planning to keep you on track and focused. This allows you to focus on many areas of your life: family/home, work/school, adventure/fun, finances, business, relationship/spiritual, health/fitness, and more! We believe all of these areas have to be in balance to achieve success. This brand-organized method, layout, and messaging has left individuals more balanced and their daily action steps more focused and intentional!

WHAT CAN WE HELP YOU ORGANIZE?

 PROJECTS

 GOALS

 FINANCES

 HEALTH

 SCHEDULE

 GROCERY LISTS

 MEAL PLANNING

 VACATIONS

 HOLIDAYS

 TO-DO LISTS

AND SO MUCH MORE! (WE SAVE YOUR LIFE! . . . NO, BUT REALLY.)

www.STARTplanner.com